The
HIDDEN PLACES
of
NORTHEAST YORKSHIRE

*including the Yorkshire Coast, Yorkshire
Moors and the Vale of York*

*Edited by
David Gerrard*

Published by:
Travel Publishing Ltd
7a Apollo House, Calleva Park
Aldermaston, Berks, RG7 8TN

ISBN 1-902-00707-7

© Travel Publishing Ltd 1998

First Published:	*1989*
Second Edition:	*1993*
Third Edition:	*1995*
Fourth Edition:	*1998*

Regional Titles in the Hidden Places Series:

Channel Islands	Devon & Cornwall
Dorset, Hants & Isle of Wight	East Anglia
Gloucestershire	Heart of England
Lancashire & Cheshire	Lake District & Cumbria
Northeast Yorkshire	Northumberland & Durham
Nottinghamshire	Peak District
Potteries	Somerset
South East	South Wales
Surrey	Sussex
Thames & Chilterns	Welsh Borders
Wiltshire	Yorkshire Dales

National Titles in the Hidden Places Series:

England	Ireland
Scotland	Wales

Printing by: Nuffield Press, Abingdon

Cartography by: Estates Publications, Tenterden, Kent

Line Drawings: Sarah Bird

Editor: David Gerrard

Cover : Clare Hackney

Born in 1961, Clare was educated at West Surrey College of Art and Design as well as studying at Kingston University. She runs her own private water-colour school based in Surrey and has exhibited both in the UK and internationally. The cover is taken from an original water-colour of the fishing port in Scarborough.

Foreword

The Hidden Places series is a collection of easy to use travel guides taking you, in this instance, on a relaxed but informative tour through the beautiful countryside, moors and coastline of Northeast Yorkshire. Our books contain a wealth of interesting information on the history, the countryside, the towns and villages and the more established places of interest in the county. But they also promote the more secluded and little known visitor attractions and places to stay, eat and drink many of which are easy to miss unless you know exactly where you are going.

We include hotels, inns, restaurants, public houses, teashops, various types of accommodation, historic houses, museums, gardens, garden centres, craft centres and many other attractions throughout Northeast Yorkshire. Most places have an attractive line drawing and are cross-referenced to coloured maps found at the rear of the book. We do not award merit marks or rankings but concentrate on describing the more interesting, unusual or unique features of each place with the aim of making the reader's stay in the local area an enjoyable and stimulating experience.

Whether you are visiting Yorkshire for business or pleasure or in fact are living in the county we do hope that you enjoy reading and using this book. We are always interested in what readers think of places covered (or not covered) in our guides so please do not hesitate to use the reader reaction forms provided to give us your considered comments. We also welcome any general comments which will help us improve the guides themselves. Finally if you are planning to visit any other corner of the British Isles we would like to refer you to the list of other *Hidden Places* titles to be found at the rear of the book.

Contents

CHAPTER ONE
The North York Moors

Beggar's Bridge, Glaisdale

Chapter 1 - Area Covered

For precise location of places please refer to the colour maps found at the rear of the book.

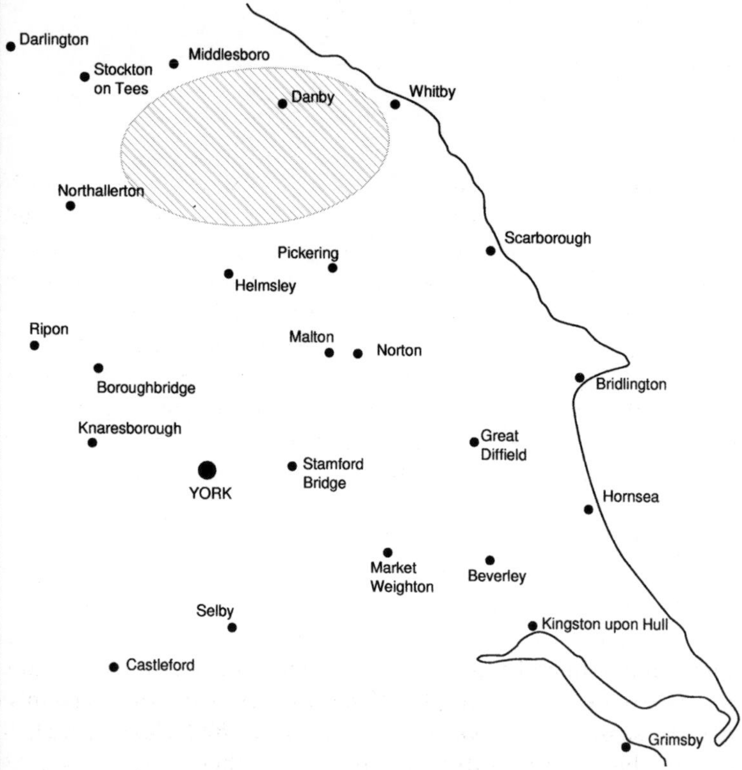

Darlington

Middlesboro

Stockton on Tees

Danby

Whitby

Northallerton

Scarborough

Pickering

Helmsley

Ripon

Malton

Norton

Boroughbridge

Bridlington

Knaresborough

Great Diffield

Stamford Bridge

YORK

Hornsea

Market Weighton

Beverley

Selby

Kingston upon Hull

Castleford

Grimsby

1
The North York Moors

Introduction

Some forty miles across and about twenty miles deep, the North York Moors encompass a remarkable diversity of scenery. There are great rolling swathes of moorland rising to 1400ft above sea level, stark and inhospitable in winter, still wild and romantic in summer, and softened only in early Autumn when they are mantled by a purple haze of flowering heather. Almost one fifth of the area is woodland, most of it managed by Forest Enterprise which has established many picnic sites and forest drives. Settlements are few and far between: indeed, there may have been more people living here in the Bronze Age (1500-500 BC) than there are now to judge by the more than 3000 *"howes"*, or burial mounds, that have been discovered. (The climate was much warmer and drier then).

Also scattered across these uplands is a remarkable collection of medieval stone crosses. There are more than thirty of them and one, the **Lilla Cross,** is reckoned to be the oldest Christian monument in northern England. It commemorates the warrior Lilla who in AD626 died protecting his King, Edwin, from an assassin's dagger. Most of them have names, - such as **Fat Betty** which has a stumpy base surmounted by the top of a wheelhead cross. Perhaps the finest of these monuments is **Ralph Cross**, high on Westerdale Moor. It stands nine feet tall at almost precisely the geographical centre of the moors and has been adopted by the North York Moors National Park as its emblem.

Wild as they look, the moors are actually cultivated land, or perhaps managed by fire is the better term. Each year, gamekeepers burn off patches of the old heather in carefully limited areas called *"swiddens"* or *"swizzens"*. The new growth that soon appears is a crucial resource for the red grouse which live only in heather moorland, eat little else but heather and find these young green shoots particularly appetising. The older heather that remains provides the birds with protective cover during their nesting season.

Just as the Yorkshire Dales have large areas of moorland, so the North York Moors have many dales - Eskdale, Ryedale, Farndale, more than a hundred of them in all. They cut deep into the great upland tracts and are as picturesque, soft and pastoral as anywhere in Yorkshire. To the west lies the mighty bulk of the Cleveland Hills; to the east the rugged cliffs of the Heritage Coast. This is marvellously unspoilt countryside, a happy state of affairs that has come about as a result of the Moors being designated a National Park in 1952, a status which severely restricts any development that would adversely affect either its natural or man-made beauty.

Two spectacularly scenic railways wind their way through this enchanting landscape. Both of them provide a satisfying and environmentally friendly way of exploring this comparatively undiscovered area, anciently known as *"Blackamor"*. The Middlesbrough to Whitby route, called the **Esk Valley Line**, runs from west to east following the course of river Esk and passing through a succession of delightful villages. The vintage steam locomotives of the **North York Moors Railway** start at Pickering and run northwards for 18 miles through Newtondale to join the Esk Valley Line at Grosmont. The dramatic route through this glacial channel was originally engineered by George Stephenson himself. During the season, the Moors Railway runs special Pullman Dining Coaches for either dinner or Sunday lunch, - a memorable experience. A very popular excursion is to take the train to Newtondale Halt and then follow one of the waymarked walks that range from easy trails to longer walks for the more adventurous. Alternatively, the Forestry Commission's **Newtondale Forest Drive** guides motorists through some splendidly rugged scenery.

Eskdale

Eskdale is the largest, and one of the loveliest, of the dales within the National Park. It is unusual in that it runs east-west, the Esk being the only moorland river that doesn't find its way to the Humber. Instead, the river winds tortuously through the dale to join the sea beneath the picturesque cliffs at Whitby. Along the way, many smaller dales branch off to the north and south, - Fryup, Danby, Glaisdale - while even narrower ones can only be explored on foot. The Esk is famed for its salmon fishing, but permits are required. These can be obtained from the local branches of the National Rivers Authority. Walkers will appreciate the Esk Valley walk, a group of ten linking walks which traverse the length of the valley.

Danby   *Map 2 ref G2*
13m E of Middlesbrough, off the A174

A visit to *The Moors Centre* at Danby Lodge provides an excellent introduction to the North York Moors National Park. The Centre is housed in a former shooting lodge and set in 13 acres of riverside, meadow, woodland, formal gardens and picnic areas. Visitors can either wander on their own along the waymarked woodland walks and nature trails or join one of the frequent guided walks. Inside the Lodge, various exhibits interpret the natural and local history of the moors, there's a bookshop stocked with a wide range of books, maps and guides, and a Tea Room serving refreshments.

Downstream from The Moors Centre is a narrow medieval packhorse bridge, one of three to be found in Eskdale. This one is known as *Duck Bridge* but the name has nothing to do with aquatic birds. It was originally called Castle Bridge but re-named after an 18th century benefactor, George Duck, a wealthy mason who paid for the bridge to be repaired. To the south of Duck Bridge are the remains of Danby Castle, now a private farmhouse and not open to the public. Built in the 14th century, and originally much larger, it was once the home of Catherine Parr, the sixth wife of Henry VIII. In Elizabethan times, the justices met here and the Danby Court Leet and Baron, which administers the common land and rights of way over the 11,000 acres of the Danby Estate, still meets here every year in the throne room. One of the court's responsibilities is issuing licences for for the gathering of sphagnum moss, a material once used for stuffing mattresses but now more commonly required for flower arranging.

In Danby village itself is the historic *Duke of Wellington Inn,* built in 1732, and reputedly named after the Iron Duke himself who used the pub as a staging post and recruiting centre. A unique plaque dating from the period was recently uncovered and now hangs in the public bar. Restoration and refurbishment has improved the facilities whilst maintaining the character and charm of this old country inn. Owned by Tony, Pat and Steve Howat, this family-run inn extends a warm welcome to all visitors. Those coming to take a glass or two of the real ale on offer in the bar can also enjoy a traditional game of dominoes or darts, as well as take the opportunity to try a tasty bar meal. The food, served both in the bar and in the

Duke of Wellington Inn

restaurant, is all home-cooked and features both traditional and imaginative dishes, including vegetarian and children's meals. It is also worth remembering that the inn has many awards for its food and drink, including recommendations by CAMRA and Egon Ronay. For those who require overnight accommodation, the Duke of Wellington has nine comfortable letting rooms available, eight of which have en suite bathrooms. The location of the inn makes it ideal for a family or activity holiday and day tickets are available from the Duke of Wellington for fishing on the nearby river Esk. *The Duke of Wellington Inn, Danby, near Whitby, North Yorkshire, YO21 2LY. Tel: 01287 660351*

Danby also gives its name to the Dale that runs south from Castleton. A narrow road runs beside Danby Beck and an even narrower lane leads to a truly Hidden Place, the bed and breakfast establishment run by Jack and Mary Lowson. Mary's association with **Sycamore House** goes back many years to just after the Second World War when, as a young girl, she came here with her family for a country holiday. Revisiting the house at Christmas and each summer throughout her childhood, the house and area became a memory until a few years ago when Mary returned with her husband Jack and purchased the then-neglected property.

Today, Sycamore House has been restored to its former glory and offers, once again, a wonderful and peaceful holiday location for families away from the hustle and bustle of everyday life. This is a happy,

Sycamore House

friendly place, offering superb bed and breakfast accommodation for a maximum of six people. There is a cosy residents lounge and plenty of local information is on hand to help visitors get the most out of their stay in the area.

Situated close to the famous Coast to Coast footpath, Sycamore House is popular with walkers and many people return here time and time again. This is an old site, - the house itself dates back to the 17th century, - and another cottage here was visited by the founder of the Quakers, George Fox. Long since demolished, Thatch House is famous within the Quaker Movement and both marriages and funerals were held there. *Jack and Mary Lowson, Sycamore House, Danby Dale, Danby, nr Whitby, North Yorkshire, YO21 2NW. Tel: 01287 660125*

Ingleby Greenhow
Map 2 ref E2

8m SE of Middlesbrough, off the B1257

West of Danby, on the very edge of the North York Moors National Park, Ingleby Greenhow enjoys a favoured position, protected from east winds by the great mass of Ingleby Moor. The beckside church looks small and unimposing from the outside, but inside there is a wealth of rugged Norman arches and pillars, the stonework carved with fanciful figures of grotesque men and animals.

Manor House Farm, set in idyllic surroundings at the foot of the Cleveland Hills, is a charming 18th century farmhouse built of Yorkshire stone, the home of Dr and Mrs Bloom. This remains a

Manor House Farm

working farm, mainly arable and sheep, but guests should not be surprised if they come across the odd wallaby or kangaroo whilst exploring the farmland. There are also deer in the nearby woods and the 300 year old pond close to the house is home to an interesting collection of wildfowl.

This is certainly a bed and breakfast establishment with a difference. It offers full board as all guests are invited to enjoy a delicious dinner in the pleasant surroundings of the cosy dining room. The full English breakfast is of an equally high standard and will certainly set all guests up for the day exploring the wonderful countryside. Also, as Manor House Farm can accommodate only six guests at a time in three comfortable bedrooms, Dr and Mrs Bloom are able to offer unique attention to all.

Not only is this a first class establishment, catering to all guests' needs, Manor House Farm can accommodate visitors' horses in stabling and a well-maintained paddock. The opportunities for riding and walking from the farm are many and well worth taking time to explore. *Manor House Farm, Ingleby Greenhow, Great Ayton, North Yorkshire, TS9 6RB. Tel: 01642 722384*

Slapewath

Map 2 ref F1

3m E of Guisborough, on the A171

The Fox and Hounds is a Country Inn and Hotel, now part of the Century Inns chain. It's an ideal choice for pleasure or business

The Fox and Hounds

purposes and guests will find the perfect blend of modern facilities and traditional comforts. The luxurious en suite bedrooms are thoughtfully furnished, very comfortable and should ensure a restful night.

For many years the Fox and Hounds has welcomed weary travellers, providing them with appetising meals in the restful bar/lounge area. The restaurant offers a full a la carte menu with an interesting variety of traditional fare, whilst a selection of daily specials and an excellent Carvery further add to the choice of mouth-watering dishes to tempt your palate. In the bar you will find a fine range of beers and cask ales. All special occasions are catered for in the function room and full banqueting facilities are available. The hotel is located on the A171 Whitby Road. *The Fox and Hounds, Slapewath, Guisborough, Cleveland, TS14 6PX Tel: 01287 632964*

A mere couple of miles from Slapewath stand the striking ruins of **Gisborough Priory** (English Heritage). Founded around 1120, Gisborough became one of the richest religious houses in the north. Today, only the east end of the priory church has survived, but it is a magnificent example of Gothic architecture, rising like a triumphal arch above the trees. In Victorian times, the priory grounds were part of a great garden, a tradition still continued with a colourful summer-long display in a large herbaceous border. An interesting survival is the octagonal two-stage dovecote where the monks

Gisborough Priory

housed the birds which would provide much of their nourishment during the winter.

Lealholm

Map 2 ref G2

8m W of Whitby, off the A171

From The Moors Centre at Danby a scenic minor road winds along the Esk Valley and brings you to the attractive village of Lealholm, its houses clustering around a 250 year old bridge over the Esk. A short walk leads to some picturesque stepping stones across the river. A much-travelled foreign journalist remarked, *"Elsewhere, you have to go in search of beautiful views; here, they come and offer themselves to be looked at"*. On one of the stone houses, now a tea room and restaurant, a carved inscription reads *Loyal Order of Ancient Shepherds* together with the date 1873 in Roman numerals. The Loyal Order ran their lodge on the lines of a men-only London club but their annual procession through the village and subsequent festivities was one of the highlights of the autumn. In recent years, Lealholm has become very popular with naturalists who come to study the wealth of trees, ferns, flowers and rare plants in the deep, dramatic ravine known as Crunkley Gill. Sadly, the ravine is privately owned and not open to the public.

The Board Inn, picturesquely situated on the banks of the River Esk, dates back to the mid 18th century. Today this wonderful free house is owned and personally run by Pauline and Clive Carruthers who came here in March 1996. Although The Board Inn was their first venture into the business, they have, without a doubt, taken to the business like ducks to water and made it a roaring success.

Outside there is a lovely beer garden where, in season, drinkers can

The Board Inn

watch the salmon and sea trout spawning and there are always lots of ducks and other water fowl. Inside the inn, which has recently been renovated, there remains an atmosphere of days gone by: brick walls, alcoves and reclaimed timbers in the ceiling. The separate dining room is similarly well decorated and is the ideal place for a cosy meal. The menu offers only the best in home cooking whilst the bar serves a range of excellent real ales.

If that was not enough, The Board Inn also has five charming guest bedrooms and more accommodation is planned. All in all this is an excellent place to visit and the pub has certainly gained an excellent reputation locally with several sports teams being based here. *The Board Inn, Village Green, Lealholm, North Yorkshire, YO21 2AJ. Tel: 01947 898279*

Glaisdale
Map 2 ref G2

8m W of Whitby, off the A171

From Lealholm, a country lane leads to Glaisdale, another pictur-esque village set at the foot of a narrow dale beside the River Esk with ***Arncliffe Woods*** a short walk away. The ancient stone bridge here was built around 1620 by Thomas Ferris, Mayor of Hull. As an

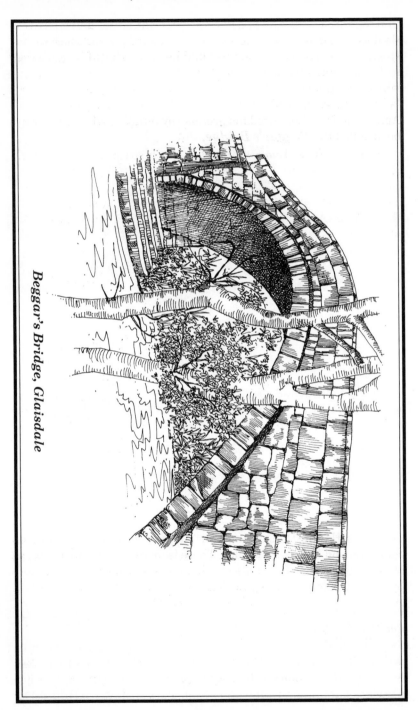

Beggar's Bridge, Glaisdale

impoverished young man, he had lived in Glaisdale and fell in love with Agnes Richardson, the squire's daughter. To see Agnes, he had to wade or swim across the river and he swore that if he prospered in life he would build a bridge here. Fortunately, he joined a ship which sailed against the Spanish Armada and captured a galleon laden with gold. Tom returned to Glaisdale a rich man, married Agnes and later honoured his promise by building what has always been called the ***Beggar's Bridge***.

The ***Arncliffe Arms***, situated in the heart of the North Yorkshire Moors, is, not surprisingly, very popular with walkers who come from all over the world to enjoy the outstanding surrounding countryside. Owned and personally run by Mike 'Lofty' Westwood, the Arncliffe Arms is the place to visit for fun and, certainly, there is plenty to enjoy here. Entertainment is of great importance and Mike

The Arncliffe Arms

organises Happy House bingo on Tuesday evenings, karaoke on Sundays, and lots more besides. There is more to smile about too, as the Arncliffe Arms also offers excellent accommodation. A visit here is sure to brighten up even the dullest day. *Arncliffe Arms, Glaisdale, North Yorkshire, YO21 2QL. Tel: 01947 897209*

Egton Bridge   Map 2 ref H2
7m SW of Whitby, off the A171

This little village tucked around a bend in the River Esk plays host each year to the famous ***Gooseberry Show***. Established in 1800, the show is held on the first Tuesday in August. It attracts entrants from all over the world who bring prize specimens in an attempt to beat the current record of 2.18oz. for a single berry. The village is dominated by the massive **Church of St Hedda** built in 1866. It has a dazzling roof painted blue with gold stars and the altar incorporates some distinguished Belgian terracotta work. Appropriately, St Hedda's is a Roman Catholic church for the martyr Nicholas Postgate was born at Egton Bridge in 1596. He was ordained as a priest in France but returned to the moors to minister to those still loyal to the outlawed Catholic faith. He travelled disguised as a jobbing gardener and eluded capture for many years but was finally betrayed for a reward of £20. He was 81 years old when he was hung, drawn and quartered at York. A sad story to be associated with such a delightful village.

Situated on the bank of the River Esk here is **The Horse Shoe Hotel**, a charming, well kept village inn offering a fine range of sales, food and accommodation. The proprietors are David and Judith Mullins who have created a really homely and welcoming atmosphere in this very well presented hostelry. Immediately striking is its neatness and old world style. Good quality home cooked food is available either from the bar snack menu or in the dining room where traditional English dishes are served as well as more exotic cuisine. The menus are complemented by an excellent wine list.

The Horse Shoe Hotel

Bed and breakfast may be enjoyed here - and what a lovely spot to stay. There are six guest bedrooms, some having en suite facilities.

Food and drink may be enjoyed in the delightful beer garden adjacent to the stream where you can relax and watch the ducks and geese busying themselves with their daily tasks. Fishing by arrangement. Pets are not allowed in the bedrooms. *The Horse Shoe Hotel, Egton Bridge, Nr. Whitby, North Yorkshire, YO21 1XE Tel: 01947 895245*

Sneaton
Map 3 ref I2

2m S of Whitby, off the B1416

Beacon Farm is an unusual and very enjoyable attraction in this beautiful part of Yorkshire. When Zoe started to make ice cream as a hobby 10 years ago, she little thought that it would turn Beacon Farm into one of North Yorkshire's premier places of interest. However, since the early days, Zoe and her husband Michael have worked hard and now provide a mecca for all ice cream lovers.

Beacon Farm

Over 30 flavours of ice cream and sorbet are now made and they are all sold at the Farm Shop and can also be tried in the wonderful Ice Cream Parlour and Tea Rooms that was opened six years ago in a converted cow byre. For ice cream lovers this is probably enough, but it was not for Zoe and Michael. Beacon Farm also has a pick your own fruit farm and there is a children's play area as well as a range of animals to meet including pot bellied pigs, donkeys, Jacob sheep and Sarah the goat. *Beacon Farm, Beacon Way, Sneaton, North Yorkshire, YO22 5HS Tel: 01947 605212*

Goathland Station

Central Moors

The area around Goathland provides some of the wildest scenery in the National Park. Murk Mire Moor, Black Rigg, Howl Moor - the very names conjure up the rigours of these upland tracts where heather reigns supreme. Even those who know the moors well treat its sudden mists and savage storms with respect. The historian of the area, Joseph Ford, recollected hearing as a child of an itinerant trader who travelled the moorland paths selling bottle corks to farmers' wives. During one particularly severe winter it was remarked that he had not paid his usual calls. The following autumn a skeleton was found on Wintergill Moor: the unfortunate victim was only *"identified by the scattered bottle corks lying nearby"*. As Ford noted, *"the story was not unusual"*.

It's a very different picture in the narrow dales that cleave their way down to the rivers. The sheltered villages here are as pretty as any in the better known western dales.

Goathland   *Map 3 ref H3*
8m SW of Whitby, off the A169

Goathland today is perhaps best known as *"Aidensfield"* - the main location for the television series *"Heartbeat"*. This attractive village 500ft up on the moors, where old stone houses are scattered randomly around spacious sheep-groomed greens, was popular long before television. Earlier visitors mostly came in order to see **Mallyan Spout**, a 70ft high waterfall locked into a crescent of rocks and trees. They were also interested in Goathland's rugged church and the odd memorial in its graveyard to William Jefferson and his wife. The couple died in 1923 within a few days of each other, at the ages of 80 and 79, and chose to have their final resting place marked by an enormous anchor.

In the award-winning **Goathland Exhibition Centre** you'll find a full explanation of the curious tradition of the Plough Stots Service, performed at Goathland every January. It's an ancient ritual for greeting the new year which originated with the Norsemen who settled here more than a thousand years ago. *"Stots"* is the Scandinavian word for the bullocks which would drag a plough through the village, followed by dancers brandishing 30-inch swords. This pagan rite is still faithfully observed but with the difference that nowadays Goathland's young men have replaced the stots in the plough harness.

The Exhibition Centre can also provide you with information about the many walks in the area and guide you to one of the oldest thoroughfares in the country, **Wade's Way**. If you believe the legend, it was built by a giant of that name, but it is actually a remarkably well-preserved stretch of Roman road.

In a splendid location overlooking the wide expanses of Goathland Moor, you will find the **Mallyan Spout Hotel**, named after the waterfall of the same name which flows into a wooded valley a short distance away. This handsome ivy-clad, stone-built hotel provides a perfect base for those interested in outdoor pursuits or the peaceful pleasures of fine food, good wine and charming hospitality.

Mallyan Spout Hotel

Inside, the atmosphere is friendly and the surroundings luxurious. There is a cocktail bar and three spacious guest lounges with views over attractive gardens to the moors and the beautiful Esk Valley beyond. Each of the 24 individually decorated bedrooms has a private bathroom, colour television, telephone and radio. Most are decorated in cottage style and have breathtaking views over the surrounding countryside and moorland. Four rooms have recently been completely refurbished and are of a particularly high quality. They are located at the rear of the hotel and have outstanding panoramic views over the moors towards Egton. Their facilities include electric curtains and full hi-fi systems. In the Coach House, two double and two twin rooms are available at ground floor level for those who find stairs a problem.

The Hotel has been owned and personally run by Judith and

Peter Heslop since the early 1970s. They ensure that their guests receive a professional standard of service which makes them feel instantly at home. The hotel restaurant is renowned for its cuisine and is open to residents and non-residents alike. The menu is long and adventurous and features freshly caught seafood from Whitby. The chef's specialities could include such delights as fresh pear poached in rosemary and lime with fresh coriander, Stilton and creme fraiche mousse for starters and sautéed medallions of monkfish with pink and green peppercorn sauce served on a bed of wild rice for a main course. All dishes are freshly cooked to order and they may require a short while to prepare. The results, however, are mouthwatering and well worth waiting for.

The privately-owned North Yorkshire Moors Railway stops at nearby Goathland station and offers fascinating excursions through heather-clad hills, wooded valleys and charming moorland villages. The Hotel also runs a programme of special weekends for the gourmet, or for those interested in such activities as hill-walking and fishing. E.T.B. 4-Crowns Commended. *Mallyan Spout Hotel, Goathland, Nr. Whitby, North Yorkshire, YO22 5AN Tel: 01947 896486. Fax: 01947 896327*

Recently frequented by the cast and crew of the popular television series *"Heartbeat"*, **The Beacon** in Goathland is a superbly sited, late Victorian substantial country house residence situated at the rear of the common, adjacent to the church. It stands in its own landscaped grounds of over an acre overlooking fields and open moorland.

The Beacon

This is an imposing house with spacious rooms, many being panelled or wainscoted with appropriate Victorian fittings. The master bedroom has unique, oak panelling dated 1631. All the bedrooms have washbasins, tea and coffee making facilities, central heating and shaver points. Bedrooms can be double, twin, family rooms or en suite. All have wonderful views.

Full English breakfast using fresh, local produce will bring back the real taste of home cooking and evening meals are available, served in the large conservatory overlooking splendid scenery. Fresh vegetables and fruit are grown in the large gardens, whilst poultry can be seen wandering around the free-range pen. This is a setting and location you will want to return to again. Open all year except for Christmas and Boxing Day. Disabled facilities are available on the ground floor. Children and controlled dogs are welcome. *The Beacon Guest House, Goathland, Whitby, North Yorkshire, YO22 5AN. Tel: 01947 896409. Fax: 01947 896431*

Barnet House Guest House sits on the edge of the village overlooking the North Yorkshire Moors Railway and Goathland Station where you will find many steam and diesel railway engines. Summer day trips by train from Goathland to Pickering are available while enjoying a nice meal and viewing the picturesque moors scenery.

Barnet House Guest House

Barnet House was built in the 16th century and was a working farm until the 1960s. It is now the home of Christine Chippindale who offers a great welcome to all her visitors. The full English breakfast is wonderful and evening meals are available by prior request. Christine has seven guest bedrooms which are all decorated in attractive and individual styles and afford views of the countryside. *Barnet House Guest House, Goathland, Whitby, North Yorkshire, YO22 5NG Tel: 01947 896201*

Just outside Goathland, you will find a particularly peaceful and relaxing hotel, the **Whitfield House Hotel,** in a very quiet location. This family run hotel with seventeen years of establishment is situated on the edge of the delightful hamlet of Darnholm. Although only a few minutes walk from Goathland the hotel occupies a very peaceful and scenic position.

Whitfield House Hotel

The handsome hotel building is a former farmhouse dating from the 17th century. Much of its original character and charm has been retained, and inside the atmosphere is truly relaxing and welcoming. The cottage-style bedrooms all have bathrooms en suite and are equipped with radio-alarms, hair dryers, TV, direct-dial telephones and drinks facilities. The standard of service is high and the full English breakfasts and table d'hote and a la carte menus offer the very best in country cooking. The hotel lies a short distance from the stepping stones at Darnholm and within easy reach of many superb woodland and moorland walks. Open 1st February until the end of November. E.T.B. 3 Crowns Commended. *Whitfield House Hotel, Goathland, North Yorkshire, YO22 5LA Tel: 01947 896215*

Beck Hole   Map 3 ref H3
7 miles SW of Whitby off the A169
Close by is the pretty little hamlet of Beck Hole. When the North Yorkshire Moors Railway was constructed in the 1830s, (designed by no less an engineer than George Stephenson himself), the trains were made up of stage coaches placed on top of simple bogies and

pulled by horses. At Beck Hole, however, there was a 1 in 15 incline up to Goathland so the carriages had to be hauled by a complicated system of ropes and water-filled tanks. (Charles Dickens was an early passenger on this route and wrote a hair-raising description of his journey). The precipitous incline caused many accidents so, in 1865, a *"Deviation Line"* was blasted through solid rock. The gradient is still one of the steepest in the country at 1 in 49, but it opened up this route to steam trains. The original 1 in 15 incline is now a footpath, so modern walkers will understand the effort needed to get themselves to the summit, let alone a fully laden carriage.

Every year, this little village plays host to the **World Quoits Championship**. The game, which appears to have originated in Eskdale, involves throwing a small iron hoop over an iron pin set about 25 feet away. Appropriately enough, one of the houses on the green has a quoit serving as a door knocker.

On the hillside, a mile or so to the west of Beck Hole, is the curiously-named **Randy Mere**, the last place in England where leeches were gathered commercially. An elderly resident of Goathland in 1945 recalled how as a young man he had waded into the lake and emerged in minutes with the slug-like creatures firmly attached to his skin. For those interested, the leeches are still there.

Rosedale Abbey
11m NW of Pickering, off the A170

Map 2 ref G3

Rosedale, to the west of Goathland, is a lovely, nine mile long steep-sided valley through which runs the River Seven. The largest settlement in the dale is Rosedale Abbey which takes its name from the small nunnery founded here in 1158. Nothing of the old Abbey has survived although some of its stones were recycled to build the village houses.

A peaceful village now, Rosedale was once crowded with workers employed in iron-ore mines on the moors. It was said that, such was the shortage of lodgings during the 1870s, 'the beds were never cold' as workers from different shifts took turns to sleep in them. The great chimney of the smelting furnace was once a striking landmark on the summit of the moor, but in 1972 it was found to be unsafe and demolished. Its former presence is still recalled at Chimney Bank where a steep and twisting road, with gradients of 1 in 3, leads up to the moor. High on these moors stands **Ralph Cross**, nine feet tall and one of more than thirty such stone crosses dotted across the moors. It was erected in medieval times as a waymark for travellers and when the North York Moors National Park was established in 1952, the Park authorities adopted Ralph Cross as its emblem.

As the name suggests, the very impressive **Coach House** was for many hundreds of years where the Lord of the Manor kept his coaches and where the coachmen would have lived. It has subsequently been refurbished and the large front windows are where the coaches would once have entered.

The Coach House

The house became an inn and restaurant only a few years ago. Tastefully converted so as not to lose its character, there are three distinct areas to the building. There is a family room with lots of pub games and where children are welcome, a bar area, and a cosy, snug restaurant area too. Since our last edition of 'Hidden Places', the inn has acquired new occupants - Bill and Jean Shepherd. Now renowned for its excellent food, the Coach House offers a set menu and extra daily specials although it is known far and wide for its authentic Indian curries. Live entertainment is a feature of this family oriented inn and can be enjoyed on various days of the week depending on the season. Bill keeps a good selection of ales and there's always a good local bitter to enjoy. *The Coach House, Rosedale Abbey, Nr. Pickering, North Yorkshire, YO18 8SD Tel: 01947 417208*

Abbey Tea Rooms, in the heart of Rosedale Abbey, was originally part of a large shop which sold mining provisions to the many hundreds of miners in the area. Those days are long gone and today the Abbey Tea Rooms offers an altogether different kind of service to those who now visit the village. Owned and run by Pat and Peter

Hainsworth, this is a real tea room: there are delicious sandwiches and salads but there are also Pat's wonderful home made cakes. The house speciality is ginger scones with ginger jam and cream, a treat not to be missed. Bright and cosy, tea is taken seriously here but most certainly enjoyed. The tea rooms are open from Easter to the end of October, but are always closed on Wednesdays.

Abbey Tea Rooms & Stores

The couple also run the adjacent *Abbey Stores* containing a small grocery department, newsagents and off licence, together with a comprehensive selection of guides and maps to support the wonderful walking situation of the area and the knowledge and guidance for visitors, an imaginative and interesting gift area completes this comprehensive business. The Stores are open throughout the year but with more restricted hours from the end of November to Easter: certainly both the Stores and the Tea Rooms are well worth a visit. *Abbey Tea Rooms and Stores, Rosedale Abbey, nr. Pickering, North Yorkshire, YO18 8SA. Tel: 01751 417475*

Hutton-le-Hole   *Map 2 ref G4*
10m NW of Pickering, off the A170

Long regarded as one of Yorkshire's prettiest villages, Hutton-le-Hole has a character all of its own. *"It is all up and down"* wrote Arthur Mee, visiting half a century ago, *"with a hurrying stream winding among houses scattered here and there, standing at all angles"*. Fifty years on, little has changed.

Ryedale Folk Museum

Facing the green is the **Ryedale Folk Museum**, an imaginative celebration of 4,000 years of life in North Yorkshire. Amongst the thirteen historic buildings is a complete Elizabethan Manor House rescued from nearby Harome and reconstructed here; a medieval crofter's cottage with a thatched, hipped roof, peat fire and garth; and the old village Shop and Post Office fitted out as it would have looked just after Elizabeth II's Coronation in 1953. Other exhibits include workshops of traditional crafts such as tinsmiths, coopers and wheelwrights, and an Edwardian photographic studio

The National Park has an Information Centre here and throughout the year there are special events such as a Rare Breeds Day and re-enactments of Civil War battles by the Sealed Knot.

The Barn Hotel stands almost next door to the Ryedale Folk Museum and was, as it name suggests, once a barn. Over 200 years old, the building was converted into a hotel in the 1960s and the present owners, Joyce and Gordon Fairhurst, came here in 1992. Charming and friendly, Joyce and Gordon ensure that all who stay here will have an enjoyable and relaxed time with all their needs looked after.

There are eight spacious and comfortable guest bedrooms, three with en suite bathrooms, and a cosy residents' lounge complete with a real fire. The hotel is open to non-residents for dinner and booking is advisable. There is also a tea room style cafe open all day. The

The Barn Hotel

charming location of this lovely hotel makes it well worth a visit and it should be noted that this is a non-smoking establishment. *The Barn Hotel, Hutton-le-Hole, North Yorkshire, YO6 6UA. Tel: 01751 417311*

Though the precise age of the **Crown Inn** is unknown, the building itself dates back a few hundred years and it retains many of the old features. Full of character, there is the original stone fireplace, decorated with bright brasses, and also a wonderful and unusual

The Crown Inn

collection of water jugs hanging from the ceiling beams. Phil Mintoft, the landlord, has been at the Crown Inn for over 12 years and it is thanks to him that the many visitors to Hutton-le-Hole have such a wonderful place to come to for excellent food and drink. As well as being known for his stock of well kept ales, Phil also provides a delicious and comprehensive menu of set dishes and daily specials that will certainly satisfy the hungriest visitor. Situated next door to the Ryedale Folk Museum, this is definitely a pub not to be missed. *The Crown Inn, Hutton-le-Hole, North Yorkshire, YO6 6UA. Tel: 01751 417343*

Anyone interested in unusual churches should make the short trip from Hutton-le-Hole to **St Mary's Church, Lastingham**, about three miles to the east. The building of a monastery here in the 7th century was recorded by no less an authority than the Venerable Bede who visited Lastingham not long after it was completed. That monastery was rebuilt in 1078 with a massively impressive crypt that is still in place - a claustrophobic space with heavy Norman arches rising from squat round pillars. The church above is equally atmospheric, lit only by a small window at one end.

Church Houses Map 2 ref F3
10m NW of Kirkbymoorside, off the A170

A couple of miles from Hutton-le-Hole, the moorland road comes to Lowna set beside the River Dove in one of the Moors most famous beauty spots, **Farndale**. In spring, some six miles of the river banks are smothered in thousands of wild daffodils, a short-stemmed variety whose colours shade from a pale buttercup yellow to a rich orange-gold. According to local tradition, the bulbs were cultivated by monks who used the petals in their medical concoctions. Yorkshire folk often refer to daffodils as Lenten Lilies because of the time of year in which they bloom. The flowers, once mercilessly plundered by visitors, are now protected by law and 2,000 acres of Farndale are designated as a local nature reserve.

In Upper Farndale you'll find a superb old country inn with all the charm, character and tradition you could wish for. **Feversham Arms** is set in picturesque surroundings in what is locally known as *"Daffodil Valley"* because of the stunning display of thousands of flowers each year. This delightful pub has been owned and personally run by Frances and Ray for the past eleven years and offers its guests the very best in comfort and hospitality. Offering a well stocked bar, this free house serves cask-brewed ale as well as stout and lager. Fine food is always available, with bar meals served every

Feversham Arms

lunchtime and evening, and you will wish to enjoy the traditional Yorkshire Sunday Lunch served in the a la carte restaurant. Wake up to superb views of the Farndale countryside from your bedroom window before sitting down and enjoying a full Yorkshire English breakfast in the stone walled and oak beamed dining room. All of the three individually styled and decorated bedrooms have a colour television and tea and coffee making facilities, and comprise of one en suite double, a family room and a twin bedded room. *Feversham Arms, Church Houses, Farndale, North Yorkshire, YO6 6LF Tel: 01751 433206*

CHAPTER TWO
The Heritage Coast

The Endeavour

Chapter 2 - Area Covered

For precise location of places please refer to the colour maps found at the rear of the book.

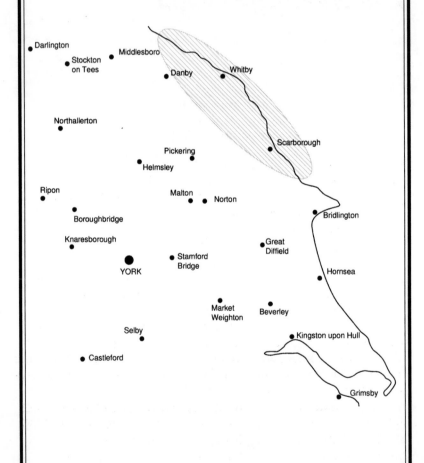

2
The Heritage Coast

Introduction

Between Saltburn and Filey lies some of the most striking coastal scenery in the country. Along this stretch of the Heritage Coast you'll find the highest cliffs in the country, a shoreline fretted with rocky coves, golden with miles of sandy beaches, a scattering of picture postcard fishing villages, and, at its heart, the historic port of Whitby dramatically set around the mouth of the River Esk.

This glorious seaboard was designated as a Heritage Coast in 1979 in recognition of its beauty and its long history. From its small ports, fishermen have for centuries sailed out in their distinctive cobles to harvest the sea; from Whitby, sturdy whaling ships set off on their dangerous and now, thankfully, abandoned trade. It was at Whitby that one of England's greatest mariners, Captain Cook, learnt his sea-faring skills and it was from here that he departed in the tiny bark, Endeavour, a mere 370 tons, on his astonishing journeys of exploration.

Further down the coast are the popular resorts of Scarborough, (where visitors were frolicking naked in the sea as early as 1735), and Filey, both of them offering long stretches of sandy beach and a huge variety of holiday entertainments.

Saltburn to Whitby

Saltburn-by-the-Sea   Map 2 ref F1
10m E of Middlesbrough on the A174

The charming seaside resort of Saltburn lies at the northern end of the Heritage Coast. It was custom-built in Victorian times and designed for affluent middle-class visitors, - so much so that in the early years excursion trains were barred from calling there. This new town, created in the 1860s by the Quaker entrepreneur Henry Pease, is set on a cliff high above a long sandy beach. To transport visitors from the elegant little town to the promenade and pier below, an ingenious water-balance tramway was constructed. It is still in use, the oldest such tramway to have survived in Britain. Saltburn's Victorian heritage is celebrated in mid-August each year with a full programme of events, many of them with the participants clad in appropriate costume. It seems appropriate, too, that such an olde-worlde town should be well-known for its many shops selling antiques and collectables.

Saltburn's Inclined Tramway

Saltburn's genteel image in Victorian times was a far cry from its notoriety in the late 18th century when it was one of the north east's busiest centres for smuggling. The *"King of the Smugglers"*, John Andrew, had his base here and during a long and profitable career was never apprehended. His story, and that of his partners in villainy, is colourfully recalled at **The Saltburn Smugglers Heritage Centre** near the Ship Inn of which Andrew was landlord.

From the seafront, a miniature railway will take you to the splendid Italian Gardens, - another Victorian contribution to the town. Here you can take tea on the lawn and explore the Woodlands Centre. set between the formal pleasure gardens and the wild natural woodlands beyond.

A few miles south of Saltburn, the outstanding *Jolly Sailor* stands amidst some of the best scenery in the country, that of the North Yorkshire Moors. It is situated on the scenic Whitby Moor Road on the A171. Owned and personally run by Charles and Sue Greener who took over this interesting pub twelve months ago, it is renowned for its good food, drink and hospitality. Dating back in parts over 300 years, it has lots of character; old beams, exposed brick walls and roaring fire. A real Yorkshire pub with a Yorkshire welcome.

The Jolly Sailor

Given its location, the Jolly Sailor has an excellent menu including many popular pub dishes. If you are really hungry then Charles has steaks to challenge most appetites! There's a small but selective wine list and, of course, a wide range of ales. Whatever the season, this is a great place to make for. *The Jolly Sailor, Whitby Moor Road, Moorsholm, Saltburn-by-the-Sea, Cleveland TS12 3LN Tel: 01287 660270*

Staithes   Map 2 ref H1
7m SE of Saltburn-by-the-Sea, off the A174
Visitors to this much-photographed fishing port leave their cars at the park in the modern village at the top of the cliff and then walk down the steep road to the old wharf. Take care - one of these nar-

row, stepped alleys is called **Slippery Hill**, for reasons that can become painfully clear. The old stone chapels and rather austere houses testify to the days when Staithes was a stronghold of Methodism.

The little port is proud of its associations with Captain James Cook. He came here, not as a famous mariner, but as a 17 year old assistant in Mr William Sanderson's haberdashery shop. James didn't stay long, leaving in 1746 to begin his naval apprenticeship in Whitby with Thomas Scottowe, a friend of Sanderson.

Staithes Harbour

Staithes is still a working port with one of the few fleets in England still catching crabs and lobsters. Moored in the harbour and along the river are the fishermen's distinctive boats. Known as cobles, they have an ancestry that goes back to Viking times. Nearby is a small sandy beach, popular with families (and artists), and a rocky shoreline extending north and south pitted with thousands of rock pools hiding starfish and anemones. The rocks here are also rich in fossils and you may even find ingots of fools gold, - actually iron pyrites and virtually worthless. A little further up the coast rises **Boulby Cliff**, at 666ft (202m) the highest point on the east coast of England.

Runswick Bay
Map 2 ref H1

9m NW of Whitby, off the A174

A little further down the coast, Runswick Bay is another pictur-esque fishing village with attractive cottages clinging to the steep sides of the cliff. This perilous position proved disastrous in 1682 when the cliff face collapsed and the whole of Runswick, with the exception of a single cottage, tumbled into the sea. A disaster fund was set up and a new village established.

At Runswick, as in most of Yorkshire's remote communities, superstition was once widespread. Even at the beginning of the 20th century, many still believed in witches, and almost everyone would avert their gaze or cross the road to avoid someone afflicted with the *"Evil Eye"*. The Revd Cooper, Vicar of Filey, visited the village at the turn of the century and came across a 'perfectly horrible superstition'. Apparently, it was considered unlucky to save a drowning man. The Vicar was told of *"men nearly dragged ashore, and then, by the advice of the elders, abandoned to their fate lest ill-fortune should result from saving them"*.

The secluded bay here once provided a perfect location for smugglers landing contraband goods. **The Runswick Bay Hotel** overlooks this old smugglers' cove and is only a few minutes walk from the beach itself.

The Runswick Bay Hotel

Originally built for the men of the local Boulby Cliff mines, the building was called *"The Sheffield"* after the road on which it stands. Throughout the summer, the exterior of the building is awash with colour and landlord Peter Folan has his work cut out watering all the hanging baskets. Inside, the Runswick Bay is equally charming: old pictures and photographs hang on the walls and shelves of books and roaring fires make for a cosy atmosphere.

As well as offering an excellent choice of ales and good home-cooking, Peter and his wife Christina, also offer guests the opportunity to take part in Murder Mysteries which they organise a couple of times each year. Excellent fun as well as offering those taking part the chance to exercise their 'little grey cells', guests can also take advantage of the first class accommodation at the Runswick Bay. For those who enjoy a less dramatic intellectual challenge there are also quiz nights each Thursday. All in all, the Runswick Bay has plenty to offer those in the area. *The Runswick Bay Hotel, Runswick Bay, North Yorkshire, TS13 5HR. Tel: 01947 841010*

Lythe *Map 3 ref H2*
4m NW of Whitby, off the A174

Perched on a hill top, Lythe is a small cluster of houses with a sturdy little church which is well worth a visit. Just south of the village is **Mulgrave Castle**, hereditary home of the Marquis of Normanby. The Castle grounds, which are open to the public, contain the ruins of Foss Castle built shortly after the Norman Conquest. Charles Dickens once spent a holiday at Mulgrave Castle and 'danced on its lawns in ecstasy at its beauty'. It's not known whether the great author witnessed the ancient custom of *"Firing the Stiddy"*. This celebrates notable events in the Normanby family and begins with dragging the anvil from the blacksmith's shop, upturning it, and placing a charge of gunpowder on its base. A fearless villager then approaches with a 20ft long metal bar, its tip red hot, and detonates the powder.

In the 1850s, Mulgrave Castle was leased by an exiled Indian Maharajah, Duleep Singh. He enjoyed going hawking on the moors in full oriental dress and the story is often told of how he had the first road between Sandsend and Whitby constructed because his elephants disliked walking along the beach. Much as one would like to believe this tale, no one has yet proved it to be true.

The Red Lion, situated on the top of the steep Lythe Bank, has been run for the last year or so by Gill and John Wood: John is a local man, well-known and regarded in the area. In such a wonderful position, the inn itself also looks a picture, with a profusion of hanging baskets, window boxes and patio tubs full of colour surrounding the entrance.

The interior of the Red Lion lives up to the expectation of its exterior: well-decorated and furnished and full of character and charm.

The Red Lion

As well as having an excellent reputation for serving good ales, Gill and John have also made the inn a popular place to come to for delicious, home-cooked food. Most importantly though, this is a friendly pub where no one is a stranger for long and, with three comfortable en suite guest bedrooms available, it is a superb place to take a short break. *The Red Lion, High Street, Lythe, North Yorkshire, YO21 3RT. Tel: 01947 893300*

Sandsend   *Map 3 ref H2*
2m NW of Whitby, on the A174

From Runswick Bay, the A174 drops down the notoriously steep Lythe Bank to Sandsend, a pretty village that grew up alongside the Mulgrave beck as it runs into the sea at 'sands end', - the northern tip of the long sandy beach that stretches some two and a half miles from here to Whitby. The Romans had a cement works nearby, later generations mined the surrounding hills for the elusive jet stone and for alum, and the Victorians built a scenic railway along the coast. The railway track was dismantled in the 1950s but sections of the route now form part of the Sandsend Trail, a pleasant and leisurely two and a half hour walk around the village which is made particularly interesting if you follow it with the National Park's booklet describing the route in your hand.

Dating back to the early 18th century, ***Estbek House Hotel*** was built for a ship's captain on the then Normanby estate and it over-

Estbek House Hotel

looks the sea. Since becoming the owners of Estbek House in 1994, Janet and Steve Cooper have made the house a very popular place indeed. On offer is luxury bed and breakfast accommodation, a first class restaurant and charming Tea Rooms. Estbek House is really well worth finding. The Georgian Room restaurant has been lovingly restored by Janet and Steve and, as its name suggests, it is an elegant Georgian room very much reflecting the age of the house. Evening dinner is by candlelight and the a la carte menu offers an excellent range of freshly prepared dishes. This delightful room is ideal for any celebration, including winter and Christmas when the log fire is burning.

During the day, the Coble Tea Room serves all manner of tasty light meals and snacks, including delicious afternoon teas complete with home-made scones. Guests can either enjoy their refreshments in the cosy tea room or outside in the flower-bordered garden overlooking the sea. Finally, Estbek House also offers luxury accommodation in a range of comfortable en suite bedrooms. This really is an excellent establishment that provides superb hospitality at reasonable prices. *Estbek House Hotel, Sandsend, North Yorkshire, YO21 3SU. Tel: 01947 893424*

Whitby

From Sandsend, the A174 skirts the shore and then passes between open fields and a breezy cliff-top Golf Course before entering one of North Yorkshire's most historic and attractive towns. Whitby is famed as one of the earliest and most important centres of Christianity in England; as Captain James Cook's home port, and as the place where, according to Bram Stoker's famous novel, Count Dracula in the form of a wolf loped ashore from a crewless ship that had drifted into the harbour. The classic 1931 film version of the story, starring Bela Lugosi, was filmed in the original locations at Whitby and there were several reports of holidaymakers startled by coming across the Count, cloaked and fanged, as he rested between takes.

High on the cliff that towers above the old town stand the imposing ruins of **Whitby Abbey**. In AD664, many of the most eminent prelates of the Christian Church were summoned here to attend the Synod of Whitby. They were charged with settling once and for all a festering dispute that had riven Christendom for generations: the precise date on which Easter should be celebrated. The complicated formula they devised to solve this problem is still in use today.

A short walk from the Abbey is **St Mary's Church**, a unique building *"not unlike a house outside and very much like a ship inside"*. Indeed, the fascinating interior with its clutter of box-pews, iron pillars and long galleries was reputedly fashioned by Whitby seamen during the course of the 18th century. The three-decker pulpit is from the same period; the huge ear trumpets for a rector's deaf wife were put in place about fifty years later. St Mary's stands atop the cliff: the old town clusters around the harbour mouth far below. Linking them are the famous 199 steps that wind up the hillside: many a churchgoer or visitor has been grateful for the frequent seats thoughtfully provided along the way.

At the foot of these steps, in the heart of the old town, stands the magnificent **Duke of York**. The 300 year old building overlooks the busy harbour and a cobbled stone road leads you to the entrance of this wonderful, historic establishment. Originally built as cottages, the inn is in a real picture postcard setting. The interior is traditional and features wooden floors, beamed ceiling and exposed brick walls. The inn is renowned for its excellent food, ales and accommodation. The menu is extensive and there are plenty of extra, daily specials. There are four well-kept real ales on tap - John Smiths,

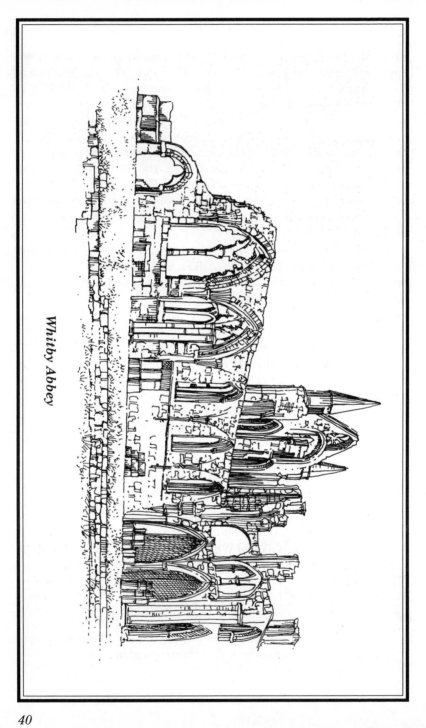

Whitby Abbey

The Duke of York

Magnet, Directors and a guest beer. The seven beautiful letting rooms have en suite facilities and are let on a room-only basis and enjoy wonderful views across the harbour. This one must not be missed. *The Duke of York, (Bottom of 199 Steps), Church Street, Whitby, YO22 4DE Tel: 01947 600234*

The old port of Whitby developed on the slim shelf of land that runs along the east bank of the river Esk, an intricate muddle of narrow, cobbled streets and shoulder-width alleys. Grape Lane is typical, a cramped little street where ancient houses lean wearily against each other. Young James Cook lived here during his apprenticeship: the handsome house in Grape Lane where he lodged is now the **Captain Cook Memorial Museum.**

Also in this ancient part of Whitby, in Sandgate, you will find the renowned studio of **Whitby Glass Ltd.**, home of the world famous *"Whitby Lucky Duck"*. The studio was founded in the early 1960s by Peter Rantell and today it is personally run by Dorothy Clegg, twice former Mayor of Scarborough. Visitors are invited to call in at the 400 year old building to observe the skilled crafts people as they draw, bend and fashion coloured glass into the intricately shaped good luck talismans. These have been exported to places as far away as Mexico and Japan, with their alleged successes including finan-

Whitby Glass Ltd

cial windfalls and the ending of a drought in southern France. *Whitby Glass Ltd., 9 Sandgate, Whitby, YO22 4DB Tel: 01947 603553*

By the early 19th century, old Whitby was full to bursting and a new town began to burgeon on the west bank of the River Esk. The new Whitby, or *"West Cliff"*, was carefully planned with the nascent industry of tourism in mind. There was a quayside walk or promenade, a bandstand, luxury hotels, and a Royal Crescent of up-market dwellings reminiscent of Buxton or Cheltenham but with the added advantage of enjoying a sea air universally acknowledged as *"invariably beneficial to the health of the most injured constitution"*.

Ashford Guest House is situated in this famous Royal Crescent, a wonderful single-sided street of late-Georgian houses which, if its builder had not got into financial difficulties, would on completion have rivalled Bath's famous Crescent. As it is, though, Royal Crescent has its own special charm and from Ashford there are views over the Crescent Gardens to the North Sea. Owned by Flora and Harry Collett, this is a family run guest house designed to offer comfortable holiday accommodation in nine en suite bedrooms. Guests can also make use of the pleasantly furnished

Ashford Guest House

guest lounge with its views over the sea front and, whilst not offering an evening meal, there is always a hearty home-cooked breakfast on offer.

Walk Whitby Way takes visitors on a walkabout to discover the folklore, myths and legends of this ancient seaport. Started in 1992, the walks are a great local attraction and have featured in television and radio travel programmes. There are several different walks which incorporate the many aspects of the town, from the Celtic Abbey to Captain Cook and Dracula. Dressed in character costume, a walk with Whitby's own Storywalker will enhance visitors' knowledge in an entertaining way, whilst the Ghost Walk tour, with the Man in Black, may be an experience that visitors never forget. Harry Collett is happy to give those interested details and he can be found at the Ashford Guest House. *Ashford Guest House, 8 Royal Crescent, Whitby, YO21 3EJ. Tel: 01947 602138*

Also to be found on Whitby's West Cliff is the attractive and well-presented *Saxonville Hotel*. Owned and run by three generations of the Newton family since 1946, guests are assured of a warm and friendly welcome and a high standard of personal service. The

Saxonville Hotel

twenty-four en suite bedrooms, which include family rooms, are tastefully decorated and furnished will all modern amenities. The restaurant is well known for its delicious cuisine and offers a choice of either table d'hote or a la carte menus. After an excellent meal, make for the comfortable lounge or bar and just relax. The Hotel is 4-Crown Commended by the English Tourist Board. *Saxonville Hotel, Ladysmith Avenue, Whitby, YO21 3HX Tel: 01947 602631. Fax: 820523.*

In a dominating position on West Cliff, a bronze statue of Captain Cook gazes out over the harbour he knew so well and nearby the huge jawbone of a whale, raised as an arch, recalls those other great Whitby seafarers, the whalers. Between 1753 and 1833, Whitby was the capital of the whaling industry, bringing home 2761 whales in 80 years. Much of that success was due to the skills of the great whaling captains William Scoresby and his son, also named William. The elder William was celebrated for his great daring and navigational skills, as well as for the invention of the crow's nest, or masthead lookout. His son was driven by a restless, enquiring mind and occupied himself with various experiments during the long days at sea in the icy Arctic waters. He is most noted for his discoveries of the forms of snow crystals and the invention of the *"Greenland"* magnet which made ships' compasses more reliable. The whaling industry is now, thankfully, long dead, but fortunately the fishing industry is not, as many of Whitby's restaurants will prove, being famous for their seafood menus.

In a splendid position on Whitby's bustling quayside there is a first-rate eating house called ***The Magpie Cafe***. The building dates from the 18th century and was once the home of the Scoresby whaling family. It was then used as a shipping office for many years before being opened as a cafe in the 1930s. The Magpie is more like

The Magpie Cafe

a top-class restaurant than a cafe, being Egon Ronay recommended and featuring in the Good Food Guide. It has also been featured as the Just a Bite Restaurant of the Year. Owners Alison McKenzie and Ian Robson have built their reputation on the quality of the food served and the service provided.

The house speciality is fresh, locally caught fish and seafood and it is said they serve the best fish and chips in the area. The menu offers a wide choice and there is much more than just fish. A variety of salads and vegetarian meals are on offer and the dessert selection is impressive to say the least! The chefs will also cater for those on special diets without a fuss. The seating areas have an atmosphere which is relaxed and welcoming with flowers on the tables and prints of old Whitby on the walls. The upper level also has magnificent views of the harbour. Open daily February to December. Opening hours vary according to season, but are generally 11.30am. to 9pm in the high season, and on Fridays and Saturdays all year. Open 11.30am-6.30pm, Sunday-Thursday, during the low season. *The Magpie Cafe, 14 Pier Road, Whitby, YO21 3PU Tel: 01947 602058*

Situated right at the end of Whitby pier, on Battery Parade, stands the **Quarter Deck,** a popular fish restaurant that has been owned and personally run by Ian and Angela Purcell for the past seven years. The building has had several different uses, - from a fisherman's shelter to a disco, but has been a successful fish restaurant for the past 33 years. The atmosphere is warm and welcoming, with traditional pine tables and chairs, attractive decor and plenty of greenery and plants to add an air of tranquillity. The menus are extensive and offer the customer a whole range of fish, meat and vegetarian dishes, served throughout the day. From fish and chips to spicy chicken wings, all the food is freshly prepared and home-cooked using only the freshest local ingredients. If you are feeling

The Quarter Deck

really hungry then you must try the 'Shipwreck Special' which contains Chicken Wings, King Prawns, Dim-Sum, Onion Balti, Stuffed Garlic Mushrooms and Vegetable Samosa, a meal fit for a king or any salty sea-dog! *Quarter Deck, Battery Parade, Whitby, YO21 3PY. Tel: 01947 604945*

One of Whitby's unique attractions is **The Sutcliffe Gallery** in Flowergate. The Gallery celebrates the great photographer Frank Meadow Sutcliffe who was born in Whitby in 1853. His studies of local people, places and events powerfully evoke the Whitby of late-Victorian and Edwardian times in photographs that are both beautifully composed and technically immaculate. Few visitors to the Gallery can resist the temptation to purchase at least one of the nostalgic prints on sale.

On the outskirts of Whitby, just off the Scarborough road, is an elegant Georgian mansion, steeped in local history, called **Larpool Hall**. The present mansion was built by Lady Jonathan Lacey in 1796 but records show that there has been a building on this site since the 12th century. In recent years, the Hall has been an orphanage, service quarters during the Second World War, and an outdoor pursuits centre until the owners, Keith and Electra Robinson, bought it in 1986.

Today, **Larpool Hall Hotel and Restaurant** offers luxurious accommodation with attentive personal service and peaceful surroundings. The hotel stands in ten acres of delightful gardens and woodland which are perfect for a relaxing or leisurely stroll. From

Larpool Hall Country House Hotel & Restaurant

the beautiful entrance hall, visitors are led to the large and elegant bedrooms. All have en suite bathrooms and all the facilities you would expect from a top class hotel. There are, in addition, ground floor bedrooms for those unable to climb the stairs. For very special occasions, the hotel boasts a romantic bridal suite on the top floor.

The public rooms include the Cholmley Lounge which overlooks the forecourt of the hotel and the Esk Valley beyond. The Dales Restaurant is also a very beautiful room and is a lovely setting for your meal. The menu reflects Electra's wide interest in, and knowledge of, cooking and ranges from traditional English and regional Yorkshire fare to more exotic dishes for the adventurous. There is always a selection of vegetarian dishes and special diets are catered for with advance notice. The Lady Jonathan Lacey Suite offers an idyllic setting for wedding receptions and other special occasions, seating up to 120 guests. E.T.B. 4 Crowns Commended: 2 Star AA + AA Rosette. *Larpool Hall Country House Hotel & Restaurant, Larpool Lane, Whitby, YO22 4ND Tel: 01947 602737. Fax: 820204.*

Whitby to Scarborough

Robin Hood's Bay   Map 3 Ref J2
5m S of Whitby, off the A171

Artists never tire of painting this *"Clovelly of the North"*, a picturesque huddle of red-roofed houses clinging to the steep face of the cliff. Bay Town, as locals call the village, was a thriving fishing port throughout the 18th and 19th centuries. By 1920 however there were only two fishing families left in the Bay, mainly because the harbour was so dilapidated, and the industry died out. Today, small boats are once again harvesting the prolific crab grounds that lie along this stretch of the coast.

Because of the natural isolation of the bay, smuggling was quite as important as fishing to the local economy. The houses and inns in the Bay were said to have connecting cellars and cupboards, and it was claimed that *"a bale of silk could pass from the bottom of the village to the top without seeing daylight"*. These were the days too when press gangs from the Royal Navy were active in the area since recruits with a knowledge of the sea were highly prized. Apparently, these mariners were also highly prized by local women: they smartly despatched the press gangs by means of pans and rolling pins.

Shipwrecks in the Bay were frequent, with many a mighty vessel tossed onto its reefs by North Sea storms. On one memorable

Robin Hood's Bay

occasion in the winter of 1881, a large brig called *"the Visitor"* was driven onto the rocks. The seas were too rough for the lifeboat at Whitby to be launched there so it was dragged eight miles through the snow and let down the cliffside by ropes. Six men were rescued. The same wild seas threatened the village itself, every storm eroding a little more of the chalk cliff to which it clings. Fortunately, Robin Hood's Bay is now protected by a sturdy sea wall.

The magnificent **Victoria Hotel** stands proudly overlooking the Bay and beyond and offers marvellous scenic views. Built in 1897, this is a hotel that really does have everything the visitor could wish for. The eleven letting rooms are of a high quality, beautifully decorated and furnished throughout. Add to this the food and drink of the highest standard and you will need to look no further. The beautiful beer gardens overlook the sea and are an ideal spot for a drink on a summer's evening. Behind the bar there are always four real ales on tap, - two are permanent and the others change regularly. The bars are open all day Friday and Saturday, and all day

The Victoria Hotel

every day in the summer season. A great establishment with a friendly service. A midday cannon is fired every Sunday from the Victoria grounds. *The Victoria Hotel, Robin Hood's Bay, Nr. Whitby, YO22 4RL Tel: 01947 880205*

Cloughton   Map 3 Ref J3
5m N of Scarborough on the A171

Cloughton village lies less than a mile from the coast and the rocky inlet of **Cloughton Wyke**. Here, in 1932, a huge whale was cast, or threw itself, ashore. Press photographers and postcard publishers rushed to the scene and paid the smallest local children they could find to pose beside the stranded Leviathan. For a while, Cloughton village was busy with a steady stream of sightseers. Their numbers quickly diminished as the six tons of blubber began to rot. In Cloughton itself, residents came to dread an east wind: it reached them only after washing over the vast hulk lying on the rocks. It's surely the worst thing that has ever happened to this pleasant little village, set around a sharp kink in the A171, where the breezes now - depending on the direction of the wind - either bring a fresh tang of ozone from the sea or a soft perfume of heather from the moors.

The Falcon Inn, a former farmhouse dating back to the late 18th century which stands on the main Scarborough to Whitby coastal road, offers some of the most spectacular views in the whole of the North Yorkshire coastal region. When Andrew Roberts first

The Falcon Inn

came here in 1989, the Falcon Inn was just another public house: today, it is one of the best inns in the area. As well as offering an excellent range of real ales in the attractive bar, the stylish restaurant - housed in the old stables - serves delicious, freshly prepared dishes that draw people from far and wide.

In the tradition of all good inns, the Falcon Inn also offers comfortable and welcoming overnight accommodation in six en suite bedrooms. Housed in the old cowsheds, the facilities are superb and, staying a little longer, guests can take advantage of the extensive grounds in which the inn is set and also wander around the recently created woodland walk. *The Falcon Inn, Whitby Road, Cloughton, YO13 0DY Tel: 01723 870717*

Burniston   Map 3 Ref J4
4m N of Scarborough on the A171

A mile or so south of Cloughton, Burniston straddles the fork of roads where the A171 and the A165 meet. Nobody famous ever lived at Burniston, no significant battle was ever fought within sight or hearing, there's not even a church. What you will find, though, is the **Harmony Country Lodge** where your hosts, Sue and Tony Hewitt, invite you to a peaceful, smoke-free retreat, surrounded by beautiful countryside on the edge of the North Yorkshire Moors National Park. The Lodge is open all year and, whatever the weather, you can be assured of a very warm welcome. Harmony Country Lodge was originally built by Charles A. Earl, an American who settled here after World War I. Formerly called *"Roundhills"*, but known locally as the *"round house"* due to its unusual octagonal design, Harmony stands in extensive private grounds, commanding beautiful panoramic views of the sea and surrounding area. The aim of

Harmony Country Lodge

Harmony is to give friendly personal service during your visit. They offer comfortable centrally heated, standard ground floor or first floor en suite bedrooms. All are attractively furnished with TV and complimentary tea and coffee making facilities. You can relax in the residents lounge or enjoy superb views from the conservatory. There is also ample parking. You can start your day with a full traditional English breakfast, and although there are plenty of restaurants to choose from nearby, an evening meal can be arranged if required. Vegetarians welcome. Cycle hire and fragrant massage are available. *Harmony Country Lodge, Limestone Road, Burniston, Scarborough, YO13 0DG. Tel: 01723 870276*

Scarborough

With its two splendid bays and dramatic cliff-top castle, Scarborough was targeted by the early railway tycoons as the natural candidate for Yorkshire's first seaside resort. The railway arrived in 1846, followed by the construction of luxury hotels, elegant promenades and spacious gardens, all of which confirmed the town's claim to the title *"Queen of Watering Places"*. The *"quality"*, people like the eccentric Earls of Londesborough, established palatial summer residences here, and an excellent train service brought countless thousands of 'excursionists' from the industrial cities of the West Riding.

Even before the advent of the railway, Scarborough had been well-known to a select few. They travelled to what was then a remote little town to sample the spring water discovered by Mrs Tomyzin Farrer in 1626 and popularised in a book published by a certain Dr Wittie who named the site *"Scarborough Spaw"*. Anne Bronte came here in the hope that the spa town's invigorating air would improve her health, a hope that was not fulfilled. She died at the age of 29 and her grave lies in St Mary's churchyard at the foot of the castle.

Scarborough Castle itself can be precisely dated to the decade between 1158 and 1168 and surviving records show that construction costs totalled £650. The castle was built on the site of a Roman fort and signal station and its gaunt remains stand high on Castle Rock Headland, dominating the two sweeping bays. The spectacular ruins often provide a splendid backdrop for staged battles commemorating the invasions of the Danes, Saxons and the later incursions of Napoleon's troops. The surrounding cliffs are also well worth exploring, just follow the final part of the famous Cleveland Way.

If you happen to be visiting the resort on Shrove Tuesday, be prepared for the unusual sight of respectable citizens exercising their ancient right to skip along the highways. This unexpected traffic hazard is now mostly confined to the area around Foreshore Road. Another tradition maintained by local people around this time is the sounding of the Pancake Bell, a custom started by the wives of the town to alert their menfolk in the fields and in the harbour that they were about to begin cooking the pancakes.

As befits such a long-established resort, Scarborough offers a vast variety of entertainment. If you tire of the two sandy beaches, there's **Peasholm Park** to explore with its glorious gardens and regular events, amongst them the unique sea battle in miniature on the lake. Or you could seek out the intellectual attractions of the **Rotunda Museum** on Vernon Road, *"the finest Georgian museum in Britain"* which includes amongst its exhibits a genuine ducking stool for 'witches'; the art collections at the **Scarborough Art Gallery**; or the futuristic world of holograms at Corrigans Arcade on Foreshore Road. **The Stephen Joseph Theatre in the Round** is well-known for staging the premiere performances of comedies written by its resident director, the prolific playwright Alan Ayckbourn. And at Scalby Mills, on the northern edge of the town, **Sea-Life** offers the chance of close encounters with a huge variety of marine creatures from shrimps to sharks, octopi to eels.

Also worth visiting is the **Wood End Museum of Natural History** on The Crescent, once the home of the eccentric Sitwell family.

There are permanent displays of their books and photographs, as well as changing exhibitions of local wildlife. The double-storied conservatory and the aquarium here are particularly interesting.

In the centre of the town is ***The Old Mill Hotel***, - a five minute walk from the station and a ten minute walk from Scarborough's outstanding shopping centre and fine sandy beach. The hotel is built in, and around, Scarborough's last remaining corn mill. Dating back to the 1700s, the mill continued to operate until 1927, though for the last years of its working life, after its six sails had been blown down in a gale, it was powered by a rare 12-horsepower gas engine.

The Old Mill Hotel

Today, the mill has been refurbished and transformed into a hotel. Inside the mill, residents and visitors can enjoy breakfast, light lunches and home baked teas in the charming and well-appointed dining room. Also within the main mill building is the hotel reception and lounge, two self-contained holiday flats, and a contemporary toy museum. The top flat, - the smaller of the two - offers fine views over and beyond the town, covering the castle and both bays. Built around the old windmill, and surrounding an attractive courtyard, are the 12 en suite bedrooms. Tastefully furnished and decorated, the ground floor rooms are well suited for wheelchair access, as are the lounge and dining room.

Also on the ground floor of the windmill, owners Angela and Roland Thompson have opened a contemporary Toy Museum for children aged from 3-93, and a play area for smaller children. Open to everyone, there is a small charge which is deducted from purchases made in the dining room. *The Old Mill Hotel, Mill Street, off Victoria Road, Scarborough, North Yorkshire, YO11 1SZ. Tel: 01723 372735*

Also situated in the heart of the town is **Louis Wine Bar,** owned and personally run by Linda and David Heppleston along with their small team, who are all very friendly and most welcoming. It is housed in the basement of a building which, like many others in the centre of Scarborough, dates back to the mid 1800s and the front facade is Grade II listed. Strictly adults only, anyone passing through the door at the bottom of the stairs is in for a lovely time.

Louis Wine Bar

Flagstone floors, soft lighting and heavy beamed ceilings all go to make a great atmosphere which makes Louis Wine Bar one of the most popular places in Scarborough. Only open in the evenings, there is a full programme of differing events which go to make this a really lively night spot. As well as serving a wide range of schnapps, cocktails, wines and the usual draught ales, the wine bar is well renowned for its excellent selection of bottled beers with over 40 from around the world at any one time. *Louis Wine Bar, 19 York Place, Scarborough, North Yorkshire, YO11 2NP. Tel: 01723 500955*

Filey *Map 8 ref K5*
7m S of Scarborough

With its six mile crescent of safe, sandy beach, Filey was one of the first Yorkshire resorts to benefit from the early 19th century craze for sea bathing. Filey's popularity continued throughout Victorian times but the little town always prided itself on being rather more select than its brasher neighbour just up the coast, Scarborough. Inevitably, modern times have brought the usual scattering of amusement arcades, fast food outlets and, from 1939 to 1983, a Butlin's Holiday Camp capable of accommodating 10,000 visitors. But Filey has suffered less than most seaside towns and with its many public parks and gardens still retains a winning, rather genteel atmosphere.

Until the Local Government reforms of 1974, the boundary between the East and North Ridings cut right through Filey. The town lay in the East Riding, the parish church and graveyard in the North. This curious arrangement gave rise to some typically pawky Yorkshire humour. If, as a resident of Filey town, you admitted that you were feeling poorly, the response might well be *"Aye, then tha'll straightly be off t'North Riding"*, - in other words, the graveyard.

Filey Bay

Just to the north of the town, the rocky promontory known as **Filey Brigg** strikes out into the sea, a massive mile-long breakwater protecting the town from the worst of the North Sea's winter storms. From the Brigg, there are grand views southwards along the six mile long bay to the cliffs that rise up to Flamborough Head and Scarborough Castle. Despite the fact that there is no harbour at Filey, it was once quite a busy fishing port and one can still occasionally see a few cobles, - direct descendants of the Viking longships that arrived here more than a millenium ago, - beached on the slipways.

Filey's parish church, the oldest parts of which date back to the 12th century, is appropriately dedicated to St Oswald, patron saint of fishermen, and the Fishermen's Window here commemorates men from the town who died at sea. At the **Filey Folk Museum**, housed in a lovely old building dating back to 1696, you can explore the town's long history, while the **Edwardian Festival**, held every June, re-creates the pleasures of an earlier, more innocent age.

Occupying a splendid sea front location with views across Filey Bay, the **Sea Brink Hotel** offers traditional family accommodation with good facilities. Proprietors Lenny Morris and Cheryl Sluder have clearly put a lot of thought and effort into making this a clean, warm and friendly establishment, well deserving of the 3-Crown Commended rating by the English Tourist Board. All the bedrooms

Sea Brink Hotel

are well presented with modern furnishings, en suite bathrooms or showers and have television, clock radio, central heating, telephone and hot drinks facilities. The residents' lounge has a sea view and there is a licensed restaurant and coffee shop. The food centres on traditional Yorkshire cuisine and the menu changes daily.

Many places of interest may be reached by car or train, whilst local leisure pursuits cater for walking, swimming, sailing, golf, fishing, windsurfing, tennis and more. Lenny and Cheryl will be happy to advise guests on all the interests and activities in the area. Ask for details of special breaks available in November and February. *Sea Brink Hotel, 3 The Beach, Filey, North Yorkshire, YO14 9LA. Tel: 01723 513257 / Fax: 01723 514139*

JR's Guest House is a comfortable family run establishment that offers the very best in warm and friendly hospitality. Jackie and Richard East bought this traditional late Victorian property just 10 years ago when it was derelict. The transformation today is complete and JR's now has four superb guest bedrooms and charmingly decorated reception rooms.

JR's Guest House

Jackie and Richard pay great attention to detail and they include some extra touches that are usually reserved for grand hotels. All the linen is monogrammed with their initials, - hence the name of the guest house, - and only the very best Denby pottery is used when serving their guests with a delicious home cooked breakfast. The couple also offer evening meals by arrangement and, being only five minutes from the beach, JR's ideal for the family. It is also worth remembering that Jackie is a linguist and is fluent in French, German and Spanish. *JR's Guest House, 5 Station Avenue, Filey, North Yorkshire, YO14 9AH. Tel / Fax: 01723 516873*

CHAPTER THREE
Herriot Country & the Hambleton Hills

Newburgh Priory

Chapter 3 - Area Covered

For precise location of places please refer to the colour maps found at the rear of the book.

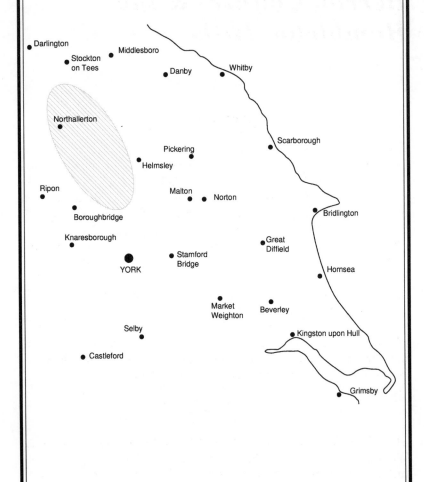

3
Herriot Country & the Hambleton Hills

Introduction

The dales strike off to the west, the moors rise to the east: in between lies this fertile corridor of rich farmland and low-lying meadows, a vast plain bisected by the Great North Road linking London and Edinburgh. For most of its life, the Great North Road has been a rocky, pot-holed and swampy obstacle course. The best stretches, by far, were those where it ran along the meticulously engineered course the Romans had built centuries earlier. It took more than eighteen hundred years for the English to realise themselves the importance of constructing viable, all-weather roads. We were, one might say, slow learners.

Passengers on the stage-coaches that lurched along the atrocious roads of 18th century England, paying the equivalent, mile for mile, of a first-class air fare today, must have longed for the next coaching hotel to appear. Fortunately, there were plenty of them to be found in the old towns along the way: towns like Thirsk.

Thirsk

Thirsk has become famous as the home of veterinary surgeon Alf Wight, better known as James Herriot, who died in 1995. In his immensely popular books, Thirsk is clearly recognisable as *"Darrowby"*. Plans are under way to convert the ivy-clad surgery at number 23, Kirkgate where he worked into a centre celebrating this modest, unassuming man whose books are known and loved around the world. Just across the road from the surgery is the birthplace of another famous son of Thirsk. The building is now the town's museum and tourist office and a plaque outside records that Thomas Lord was born here in 1755: thirty years later he was to create the famous cricket ground in Marylebone that took his name. A more recent celebrity whose home is in Thirsk is Bill Foggitt, renowned for his weather forecasts based on precise observations of nature.

James Herriot's Surgery

This pleasant small town of mellow brick houses has a sprawling Market Place and a magnificent 15th century church which is generally regarded as the finest parish church in North Yorkshire. It was here that the real life *"James Herriot"* married his wife, Helen. **Cod Beck**, a tributary of the River Swale, wanders through the town, providing some delightful - and well-signposted - riverside walks. Thirsk appeared in the Domesday Book not long after William the Conqueror had granted the Manor of Thirsk to one of his barons, Robert de Mowbray. The Mowbrays became a powerful family in the area, a fact reflected in the naming of the area to the north and west of Thirsk as the Vale of Mowbray. In the early 1100s the family received permission to hold a market at Thirsk but then blotted their copybook by rebelling against Henry II in 1173. The rebellion failed and their castle at Thirsk was burnt to the ground. Not a trace of it remains. The market however is still thriving, held twice-weekly on Mondays and Saturdays. An old market by-law used to stipulate that no butcher be allowed to kill a bull for sale in the market until the beast had been baited by the town dogs. The by-law has long since been abandoned, and the bull-ring to which the animal was tethered has also disappeared.

On the edge of the town is the ***Trees to Treske Visitor Centre***, an imaginative exhibition exploring how trees grow, the character of different woods and examples of the cabinet maker's craft. Nearby is ***Thirsk Racecourse***, known to devotees of the turf as the *"Country Racecourse"*. There are around 12 race meetings each year, all well attended, especially by visitors wishing to sample an intrinsic part of Yorkshire life. Travelling through the areas between the Dales and the North York Moors, one is constantly reminded of the great tradition of horse-breeding that the county is famous for. The tradition runs deep: - even the long flat straight stretch of main railway line between York and Darlington is known as the *"Racecourse"*.

Another great tradition in Thirsk is clockmaking whose history in the town can be traced back to the early 1700s. Five years ago, Steve Aldridge and his brother-in-law Bill Bradbury opened ***Hickory Dickory Clocks***. Their tiny shop is crowded with grandfather clocks, mantel clocks and wall clocks on every available surface, all ticking

Hickory Dickory Clocks

and chiming independently, with no regard for the real time in the real world.

Steve and Bill make, sell, restore and repair clocks from all over the world, ranging from small carriage clocks to long case clocks: you can guarantee that their knowledge and their fascination with the subject of time will become quite infectious. The couple have recently made a limited edition of 100 long case (grandfather to you and me) clocks dedicated to the memory of the town's most famous vets, Alf Wight (James Herriot), and his partner Donald Sinclair (Siegfried). You can visit this intriguing shop and watch the clockmasters at work every day except Wednesday, and also Sundays except in August, though Steve and Bill will open by appointment. *Hickory Dickory Clocks, 27 Market Place, Thirsk, North Yorkshire, YO7 1HD. Tel: 01845 526393. Fax: 01845 527041*

Around Thirsk

A couple of miles south of Thirsk, set within one and a half acres of beautiful gardens and surrounded by fifteen acres of rolling parkland, stands the secluded *Spital Hall*. This graceful Victorian home is owned and personally run by Ann and Robin Clough, a welcoming couple who ensure that their visitors enjoy good food and congenial hospitality during their stay. All of the three guest bedrooms are elegantly decorated and furnished with heavily cloth-draped period

Spital Hall

beds, have magnificent views and, in one bedroom, a Bechstein piano. Each of the comfortable rooms has the usual home comforts including a few well thought of extras which will ensure that your break at Spital Hill will be a memorable one.

The half timber panelled dining room with grandfather clock and Victorian marbled fireplace is the perfect place to enjoy Ann's mainly traditional English fare which is complemented by a small but carefully chosen range of wines. All the bread that Ann uses is home baked, and the evening menu uses only the freshest seasonal garden produce to create such mouth-watering dishes as *"Pork fillet in port wine sauce with dates and walnuts"*. Close to the main house, luxuriously and skilfully refurbished, stands a self-catering holiday cottage that can sleep up to four guests. This enchanting cottage retains many of its original features, and great care has been taken to keep the decor and furnishings in period whilst still offering all modern conveniences. You can reach this tranquil hidden place by a private road marked by two short white posts on the west side of the A19 Thirsk to York road, one mile south of the A19/A170/A168 intersection. *Spital Hill, Thirsk, North Yorkshire, YO7 3AE. Tel: 01845 522273*

Sion Hill Hall, about four miles northwest of Thirsk, is celebrated as the *"last of the great country houses"*. Its light, airy and well-proportioned rooms, all facing south, are typical of the work of the celebrated Yorkshire architect, Walter Brierley - the *"Lutyens of the North"*. He completed the building in 1913 for Percy Stancliffe and his wife Ethel, the wealthy daughter of a whisky distiller. The rooms haven't altered one bit since they were built, but the furniture and furnishings certainly have. In 1962, the Hall was bought by Herbert Mawer, a compulsive but highly discerning collector of antiques. During the twenty years he lived at Sion Hill, Herbert continued to add to what was already probably the best collection of Georgian, Victorian and Edwardian artefacts in the north of England. Furniture, paintings, porcelain, clocks (all working), ephemera, crowd the twenty richly furnished rooms and make Sion Hill a delight to visit. A recent addition to the many sumptuous displays is a charming exhibition of dolls from the early 1900s.

In the Hall's Victorian Walled Garden is another major attraction, - *Falconry U.K.'s Bird of Prey and Conservation Centre*. More than eighty birds from 34 different species have their home here: owls, hawks, falcons, buzzards, vultures and eagles from all around the world. At regular intervals throughout the day these fierce-eyed, sharp-beaked predators behave in a remarkably docile and co-operative way as they take part in fascinating flying demonstrations.

Holme-on-Swale   *Map 1 ref C4*
6m W of Thirsk, off the B6267

The narrow, winding country lane that leads to Holme-on-Swale passes through the tiny village and comes to a full stop at the River Swale. Here, an embankment protects the meadows from flooding and also provides a tranquil riverside walk stretching southwards for some five miles.

The former gatehouse to a large country house, *Glen-free* dates back, in parts, to the mid 17th century. Today this single storey house is the home of Julie and Michael Bailes, a charming and friendly couple who offer wonderful bed and breakfast accommodation in two delightful bedrooms. The couple have lived here for over 35 years and, as well as having a detailed knowledge of the surrounding countryside and its various attractions, they have also put a lot of work into making both their house and garden an absolute picture.

Glen-free

Cosy and comfortable inside, Glen-free has a most magnificent garden that is a riot of colour for many months of the year. Well cared for and with many interesting features, guests are free to use the garden and children will be particularly delighted with the wildlife pond. Though Julie and Michael do not offer an evening meal, breakfast is outstanding and will certainly set guests up for a day out in the countryside. Both children and pets are welcome, and it should be remembered that this is a no smoking establishment. *Glen-free, Holme-on-Swale, Nr. Swinderby, North Yorkshire, YO7 4JE. Tel: 01845 567331*

Londonderry   Map 1 ref B4
8m SW of Northallerton, off the A1

Situated in three acres of grounds, mid-way between the old and new A1 at Londonderry, is the impressive *Tatton Lodge*. Formerly a farmhouse, then an alehouse and then an inn, it is now a private house that offers first class bed and breakfast accommodation. It is owned and personally run by Denise and Jim Bleasdale whose love of horses is very apparent from the moment you arrive. Jim was a flat race jockey for over 20 years, and Denise is also a keen horse-woman as you will see from some of their horses in the adjoining pasture.

Tatton Lodge

There are six letting rooms in all, three of which are houses in the recently-converted stables, whilst the others are located in the main house. All of the rooms are of an excellent quality, with the bed-rooms in the main house boasting magnificent views towards the North York Moors. This is an outstanding establishment where you can enjoy the first class facilities and be truly pampered amidst the surrounding peace and tranquillity. *Tatton Lodge, Londonderry, nr. Northallerton, North Yorkshire, DL7 9NF. Tel/Fax: 01677 422222*

Conveniently situated just off the A1, *Little Holtby* provides excellent overnight accommodation both for through travellers and for those looking for a touring base in the beautiful Vale of York.

Little Holtby

This fully refurbished farmhouse has lovely gardens and provides spectacular views across the rolling countryside towards Pen Hill. Owner Dorothy Hodgson always provides her guests with a warm welcome and superb Yorkshire hospitality. She has four beautifully decorated guest rooms available, three with en suite facilities and the fourth with its own private bathroom. All are immaculately furnished and appointed to a good modern standard and particularly attractive are the wooden floors and furniture throughout the establishment. For those interested in clocks, Dorothy has a wonderful collection, including some Grandfather Clocks, which is displayed around the house. As well as offering an excellent breakfast each morning, guests can also take advantage of the packed lunches and filled flasks that are on offer and, at the end of the day, Dorothy also offers an evening meal by prior arrangement. Open all year round, Little Holtby is a wonderful place to stay and children are always welcome. *Little Holtby, Leeming Bar, Northallerton, North Yorkshire, DL7 9LH. Tel: 01609 748762*

Northallerton and the Vale of Mowbray

The county town of North Yorkshire, Northallerton has the broad High Street, almost half a mile long, typical of the county's market towns. In stage coach days the town was an important stop on the route from Newcastle to London and several old coaching inns still stand along the High Street. The most ancient is **The Old Fleece**, a favoured drinking haunt of Charles Dickens during his several visits to the town. It's a truly Dickensian place with great oak beams and a charming olde-worlde atmosphere. The Old Fleece recalls the great days of the stage coach which came to an abrupt end with the arrival of the railway. One day in 1847, a coach called the Wellington made the whole of the 290 mile journey from Newcastle to London, via Northallerton, completely empty. The era of this romantic - if uncomfortable and extremely expensive - mode of transport was over.

Northallerton has many old buildings of interest, including an ancient Grammar School whose history goes back to at least 1322. The school was rebuilt in 1776 at the northern end of the High Street - a building that is now a solicitors' office. By the end of the 19th century the school had *"no great reputation"* and by 1902 only thirteen pupils were registered. Things went from bad to worse the next year when the headmaster was convicted of being drunk and disorderly. Fortunately the school, now Northallerton College and in new buildings, has recovered its reputation for academic excellence.

The town also boasts a grand medieval church, a 15th century almshouse and, of more recent provenance, a majestic County Hall built in 1906 and designed by the famous Yorkshire architect Walter Brierley. The oldest private house in Northallerton is **Porch House**, which bears a carved inscription with the date 1584. According to tradition, Charles I came here as a guest in 1640 and returned seven years later as a prisoner.

Masham House

Conveniently situated just two minutes walk from the centre of Northallerton stands the impressive **Masham House**. This fine house dates back to the mid 19th century and has been owned and run for the past three years by Judy and Stan Pennington, a welcoming couple who offer their guests first class bed and breakfast accommodation. Back in the 1950s the first floor letting room was once used as a small nursery school, so that should give some indication of the generous size of the bedrooms. Both of the two en suite guest bedrooms are attractively decorated and furnished throughout, whilst the exposed wooden floored dining room is the perfect place to enjoy a traditional English breakfast before embarking on your day's excursions. *Masham House, 18 South Parade, Northallerton, North Yorkshire, DL7 8SG Tel: 01609 771541*

Two miles north of the town, a stone obelisk beside the A167 commemorates the **Battle of the Standard**, fought here in 1138. It was one of the countless conflicts fought between the English and the Scots, and also one of the bloodiest with more than 12,000 of the Scots, led by King David, perishing under a rain of English arrows. The battle took its name from the unusual standard raised by the English: the mast of a ship mounted on a wagon and, crowning its top, a pyx containing the consecrated Host.

Osmotherley
Map 1 ref D3

6 miles E of Northallerton off the A19

Mount Grace Priory, (English Heritage & National Trust), near the village of Osmotherley about 7 miles northeast of Northallerton, is quite unique amongst Yorkshire's ecclesiastical treasures. The 14th century building set in tranquil surroundings was bought in 1904 by Sir Lothian Bell who decided to rebuild one of the well-preserved cells, a violation of the building's integrity that would provoke howls of outrage from purists if it were proposed today. When English Heritage inherited the Carthusian Priory, however, it decided to go still further by reconstructing other outbuildings and filling them with replica furniture and artefacts to create a vivid impression of what life was like in a 14th century monastic house. The Carthusians were an upper class order whose members dedicated themselves to solitude, - even their meals were served through an angled hatch so they would not see the servant who brought them. Most visitors find themselves fascinated by Mount Grace's sanitary arrangements which were ingeniously designed to take full advantage of a nearby spring and the sloping site on which the Priory is built.

Potto
Map 1 ref D3

11m NE of Northallerton, off the A172

Situated within picturesque farmed parkland on the western edge of the North York Moors National Park and standing in its own peaceful gardens and grounds is the serene **Potto Grange**. This ivy covered, Grade II Listed Georgian farmhouse has been in the same family for the past 250 years and today is owned by Major and Mrs

Potto Grange

Julian Kynge. Potto Grange has offered accommodation for the past 3 years and provides its guests with the opportunity of sampling the very best in country living. Guests have their own beautifully furnished drawing room with grand piano, and a spacious and sunny en suite bedroom complete with all the comforts of home and more.

There is a hard tennis court and croquet lawn set within the grounds and children can enjoy a game of table tennis in the old granary. Fishing can also be enjoyed in the private lake, just 2 miles away, where you will find a good supply of Rainbow Trout in season. All of the meals served at Potto Grange have been created using only the freshest seasonal ingredients from the country house's large fruit and vegetable garden, though prior arrangement is needed for evening meals. The traditional grassland farm has some rare white Galloway cattle as well as bronze turkeys, guinea fowl and white silkie hens, - perfect for those freshly boiled eggs for breakfast. This hidden gem is a little difficult to find so we recommend that if you are travelling north along the A19, take the A172 towards Stokesley, after a couple of miles turn left at the Potto sign, follow this road for a quarter of a mile, then turn right at the white gate and railings. *Potto Grange, Nr. Northallerton, North Yorkshire, DL6 3HH. Tel: 01642 700212*

Great Ayton
Map 2 ref E2

6m SE of Middlesbrough, on the A173

This appealing village, set around the River Leven, is an essential stopping point for anyone following the Captain Cook Country Tour, a 70 mile circular trip taking in all the major locations associated with the great seafarer. Cook's family moved to Great Ayton when he was eight years old and he attended the little school which is now the ***Captain Cook Schoolroom Museum***. Here you will find a fascinating re-creation of the village in which he spent some of his most formative years. The house in which the Cook family lived is sadly no longer here. In 1934 it was transported to Australia brick by brick, together with the climbing plants that covered them, and re-erected in Fitzroy Park, Melbourne. A cairn of stones is all that remains to mark the site. A much more impressive monument is the 60ft obelisk to Cook's memory erected on Easby Moor above the village by Robert Campion, a Whitby banker, in 1827. It can only be reached by a steepish climb on foot but it is well worth making the effort: from the base of the monument there are stupendous views over the Moors, the Vale of Mowbray and across to the oddly shaped hill called Roseberry Topping. The loftiest of the Cleveland Hills and sometimes called the Matterhorn of Yorkshire, Roseberry's summit towers 1000ft above Great Ayton.

Originally the village dairy for over 30 years, ***The Old Dairy Tea Rooms*** stands in this pretty village in the depths of the Yorkshire countryside. The building dates back to the turn of the century when it was a row of three cottages, but it is today the home of a traditional English tea room where all the cakes and fancies are freshly baked on the premises. Owned and personally run by Rebecca

The Old Dairy Tea Rooms

and Richard, the tea room is open 7 days a week throughout the summer from 10am until 5pm, serving delicious light lunches all day, with home made cakes and cream teas being specialities of the house. The atmosphere is relaxed and informal, classical and jazz music play quietly in the background whilst you sit and peruse the comprehensive menu which also contains a wide range of home made jams available for you to purchase and take away, as are the fresh baked scones and cakes. Rebecca and Richard also run an outside catering service that offers its clients lunches, suppers, dinners, parties, receptions and teas, all at very reasonable rates. There is pleasant courtyard seating for the summer months, and there is full disabled access and toilet facilities. *The Old Dairy Tea Rooms, 5 Park Square, Great Ayton, North Yorkshire, TS9 6BP. Tel: 01642 722646*

The Hambleton Hills

For one of the grandest landscape views in England, go to the top of Sutton Bank in the Hambleton Hills and look across the vast expanse of the Vale of York to the Pennine hills far away to the west. James Herriot called it the *"finest view in England"*. He knew this area well since his large veterinary practice covered the farms from here right over to the Dales. A continuation of the Cleveland Hills, the Hambleton Hills themselves lead into the Howardian Hills: together they form the mighty southwest flank of the North York Moors.

There's a National Park Information Centre at the summit of Sutton Bank and a well-marked Nature Trail leads steeply down to, and around, **Lake Gormire**, an Ice Age lake trapped here by a landslip. Gormire is one of Yorkshire's only two natural lakes, the other being Semerwater in Wensleydale. Gormire is set in a large basin with no river running from it: any overflow disappears down a *"swallow hole"* and emerges beneath White Mare Cliffs.

Sutton Bank used to be a graveyard for caravans because of its steep (1 in 3) climb and sharp bends. On one July Saturday in 1977, some thirty vehicles broke down on the ascent and five breakdown vehicles spent all day retrieving them. Caravans are now banned from this route. Sutton Bank may be tough on cars but its sheer cliffs create powerful thermals making this a favoured spot for gliders and bright-winged hang-gliders.

Boltby *Map 1 ref D4*

5m NE of Thirsk, off the A170

Boltby is an engaging village tucked away at the foot of the Hambleton Hills, close to where the oddly-named Gurt of Beck tumbles down the hillside and, depending on how much rain has fallen on the moors, passes either under or over a little humpback bridge. On the plain below is Nevison House, reputed to be the home of the 17th century highwayman, William Nevison, *"Swift Nick"* as Charles II dubbed him. Some historians claim that it was *"Swift Nick"*, not Dick Turpin, who made the legendary ride on Black Bess from London to York to establish an alibi.

From Boltby, a minor road climbs up Sneck Yate Bank to *Low Paradise,* the charming home of Thelma Todd. This is very much a hidden place, off the beaten track and surrounded by some wonderful countryside. Close to both the Cleveland Way and the White Rose Walk, this mid 17th century farmhouse was built close to an old drovers' road. Once found, it is easy to see how the house got its name: the views in all directions, over the Vale of York and the Hambleton Hills, are spectacular. The tranquillity and peace of Low Paradise is also well worth experiencing and, for those interested in the life of the famous vet, James Herriot, the farm was within his local practice.

Low Paradise

Thelma has been offering bed and breakfast accommodation from her home for the last 15 years and is something of an expert. The four guest rooms are very comfortable and beautifully decorated to a high standard, whilst downstairs, along with the modern conveniences of the late 20th century, are many of the house's original features. It is worth remembering that Thelma can only take six guests at any one time and is always happy to provide an evening meal by prior arrangement. Thelma is also happy to provide directions to the house which lies to the north of Boltby. *Low Paradise, Boltby, Nr. Thirsk, North Yorkshire, YO7 2HS Tel: 01845 537253*

Kilburn

Map 1 ref D5

5 miles E of Thirsk off the A170

A few miles south of Low Paradise, a minor road off the A170, signposted to Kilburn, leads to the famous **White Horse** inspired by the prehistoric White Horse hill-carving at Uffingham in Berkshire. John Hodgson, Kilburn's village schoolmaster, enthused his pupils and villagers into creating this splendid folly in 1857. It is 314ft long and 228ft high and visible from as far away as Harrogate and Otley. Unlike its prehistoric predecessor in Berkshire, where the chalk hillside keeps it naturally white, Kilburn's *"White"* horse is scraped from grey limestone which needs to be regularly groomed with lime-washing and a liberal spreading of chalk chippings.

Just beyond the White Horse is Kilburn village, the home of one of the most famous of modern Yorkshire craftsmen, Robert Thompson, - the *"Mouseman of Kilburn"*. Robert's father was a carpenter but he apprenticed his son to an engineer. At the age of 20 however, inspired by seeing the medieval wood carvings in Ripon Cathedral, Robert returned to Kilburn and begged his father to train him as a carpenter. An early commission from Ampleforth Abbey to carve a cross settled his destiny: from then until his death in 1955 Robert's beautifully crafted ecclesiastical and domestic furniture was in constant demand. His work can be seen in more than seven hundred churches, including Westminster Abbey and York Minster. Each piece bears his signature, - a tiny carved mouse placed in some inconspicuous corner of the work. According to a family story, Robert adopted this symbol when one of his assistants happened to use the phrase *"as poor as a church mouse"*. (Signing one's work wasn't an entirely new tradition: the 17th century woodcarver Grinling Gibbons' personal stamp was a pod of peas). Robert Thompson's two grandsons have continued his work and their grandfather's former home is now both a memorial to his genius and a showroom for their own creations.

Coxwold

Map 2 ref E5

9m SE of Thirsk, off the A19 or A170

Coxwold enjoys a particularly lovely setting in the narrow valley that runs between the Hambleton and Howardian Hills. At the western end of the village stands the 500 year old **Shandy Hall**, home of Laurence Sterne, vicar of Coxwold in the 1760s. Sterne was the author of *"Tristram Shandy"*, that wonderfully bizarre novel which opened a vein of English surreal comedy leading directly to The Goons and the Monty Python team. The architecture of the Hall, Tudor in origin, includes some appropriately eccentric features - strangely-shaped balustrades on the wooden staircases, a Heath Robinson kind of contraption in the bedroom powder-closet by which Sterne could draw up pails of water for his ablutions, and a tiny, eye-shaped window in the huge chimney stack opening from the study to the right of the entrance. A more conventional attraction is the priceless collection of Sterne's books and manuscripts.

The Revd Sterne much preferred the cosmopolitan diversions of London to the rustic pleasures of his Yorkshire parish and rarely officiated at the imposing church nearby with its striking octagonal tower, three-decker pulpit and Fauconberg family tombs. A curiosity here is a floor brass in the nave recording the death of Sir John Manston in 1464. A space was left for his wife Elizabeth's name to be added at a later date. The space is still blank. Outside, against the wall of the nave, is Sterne's original tombstone, moved here from London's Bayswater when the churchyard there was deconsecrated in 1969.

The School House, owned by Jean and John Richardson, is a very well appointed 17th century cottage of considerable character

The School House

and charm. It was once a coaching house and now under their personal supervision offers accommodation of the highest quality and is also noted for its home cooking. School House has three double bedrooms, pleasantly decorated and containing many pieces of period furniture. Each is equipped with wash basins, TV and drinks facilities. There are two guest bathrooms with showers that are close to the bedrooms. Packed lunches can be provided and evening meals are available on request. Part of the house opens as a tea room each afternoon from Easter to the end of October. The menu offers traditional afternoon teas and all the food is freshly prepared and home made. *School House, Coxwold, North Yorkshire, YO6 4AD. Tel: 01347 868356*

Just to the south of Coxwold is ***Newburgh Priory***, founded in 1145 as an Augustinian monastery and now a mostly Georgian country house with fine interiors and a beautiful water garden. Since 1538, the Priory has been the home of the Fauconberg family. An old tradition asserts that Oliver Cromwell's body is interred here. Cromwell's daughter, Mary, was married to Lord Fauconberg and when Charles II had her father's corpse hanged at Tyburn and his head struck off, Lady Fauconberg claimed the decapitated body,

Newburgh Priory

brought it to Newburgh and, it is said, buried the remains under the floorboards of an attic room. The supposed tomb has never been opened, the Fauconbergs even resisting a royal appeal from Edward VII when, as Prince of Wales, he was a guest at the Priory. The house, which is still the home of the Earls of Fauconberg, and its extensive grounds are open to the public during the spring and summer months.

From Coxwold, follow the minor road northeastwards towards Ampleforth. After about 2 miles, you will see the lovely, cream-coloured ruins of **Byland Abbey**. The Cistercians began building their vast compound in 1177 and it grew to become the largest Cistercian church in Britain. Much of the damage to its fabric was caused by Scottish soldiers after the Battle of Byland in 1322. The English king, Edward II had been staying at the Abbey but fled after his defeat, abandoning vital stores and priceless treasures. In a frenzy of looting, the Scots made off with everything the king had left and ransacked the Abbey for good measure. The ruined west front of the Abbey, although only the lower arc of its great rose window is still in place, gives a vivid impression of how glorious this building once was.

Ampleforth
Map 2 ref E5
10m SE of Thirsk, off the A170

Set on the southern slopes of the Hambleton Hills, Ampleforth is perhaps best known for its Roman Catholic public school, **Ampleforth College**, established by the Benedictine community that came here in 1809, fleeing from persecution in post-revolutionary France. The monks built an austere-looking **Abbey** in the Romanesque style amongst whose treasures are an altar stone rescued from Byland Abbey and finely crafted woodwork by the *"Mouseman of Kilburn"*, Robert Thompson.

Just down the road from Ampleforth College is **The White Swan**, a popular pub with a real Yorkshire owner, Gary Benson. Since coming here in the late 1980s, and being the proud owner of the White

The White Swan

Swan from the end of 1994, Gary has transformed this charming 17th century coaching inn, turning it into a thriving inn which reflects his open and friendly personality. As well as enjoying a pint or two of excellent John Smith's Ale, there is a very varied wine list and the meals served here have become legendary in their own right. Back in the 1970s, the White Swan was considered a pioneer in the area for its basket meals, - something of a cliche in today's sophisticated world, - but the pub has not rested on its laurels and the menu is imaginative and interesting. Renowned for its large steaks and mixed grills, no one visiting the White Swan will go hungry. There is a cosy restaurant for more formal dining but meals can be taken in all parts of the pub, including the neat and tidy patio area. This is an excellent and honest pub which offers a real taste of Yorkshire. *The White Swan, Ampleforth, North Yorkshire, YO6 5EL. Tel: 01439 788239*

Easingwold

Map 2 ref E6

8m SE of Thirsk, off the A19

This agreeable market town was once surrounded by the Forest of Galtres, a vast hunting preserve of Norman kings. It lies at the foot of the Howardian Hills, an Area of Outstanding Natural Beauty covering 77 acres of woods, farmland and historic parkland. Easingwold's prosperity dates back to the 18th century when it flourished as a major stage coach post, - at that period the town could offer a choice of some 26 public houses and inns. Until the recent construction of a bypass the old town was clogged with traffic but it

Market Place, Easingwold

is now a pleasure again to wander around the market place with its impressive Market Cross and, nearby, the outline of the old bull-baiting ring set in the cobbles. Easingwold used to enjoy the distinction of having its own private railway, a two and a half mile stretch of track along which it took all of ten minutes to reach the main east coast line at Alne. Older residents fondly remember the ancient, tall-chimneyed steam locomotive that plied this route until its deeply regretted closure to passenger traffic in 1948.

The Angel public house, a black and white building dating back to the 17th century, overlooks the market square in the centre of the town. In the pleasant and cosy atmosphere, enhanced by brick fireplaces and original oak beams, festooned with gleaming horse brasses and old sporting prints, Barry Hooper offers a warm welcome. This popular, friendly pub serves fine ales and features guest beers but it is perhaps better known for the delicious menu that is served here every lunchtime and evening (except Sunday evening). Interesting and tasty, the two menus are supplemented by the ever-changing list of daily specials. Barry owns a couple of racehorses so

The Angel

guests should not be too surprised when they bump into the occasional jockey or trainer. The Angel is also a popular haunt of the local cricket and rugby teams and most evenings there's a pub game, such as darts or dominoes, being played. This is a cracking place that is well worth a visit. *The Angel, Market Place, Easingwold, North Yorkshire, YO6 3AA. Tel: 01347 821605*

CHAPTER FOUR
The Vale of Pickering

Kirkham Priory

Chapter 4 - Area Covered

For precise location of places please refer to the colour maps found at the rear of the book.

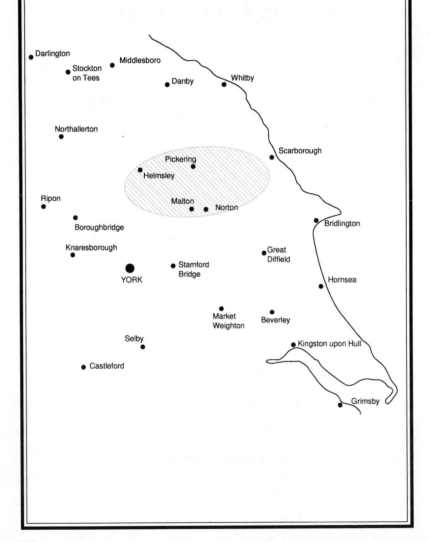

4
The Vale of Pickering

Introduction

Not all that long ago, the Vale of Pickering was the Lake of Pickering, an immense stretch of water far larger than any English lake today, about 32 miles long and four to eight miles wide. As the Ice Age retreated, the waters gradually drained away leaving a low-lying plain of good arable soil based on Kimmeridge clay. Much of it remained marshy however and at Star Carr, near Seamer, archaeologists have uncovered a late Stone Age lake community, dating back some 7,500 years, where the houses were built on stilts above the water. Sadly, the remains of this fascinating excavation lie on private land and are not open to the public. It is only in comparatively recent times that the Vale has been properly drained, which explains why most of the towns and villages lie around its edge in a rough kind of horseshoe formation.

For much of its length, the Vale is watered by the River Derwent, which was also powerfully affected by the changes that occurred during the Ice Age. Originally it entered the sea near Scarborough but an Ice Age glacier blocked that outlet. The Derwent still flows to within a mile and a half of Scarborough, but now turns abruptly and makes a 90-mile detour through the vale and then southwards to join the River Ouse near Howden.

The main traffic artery through the vale is the Thirsk to Scarborough road, the A170, which in summer peak periods can become very congested. But you only have to turn off this busy thoroughfare to find yourself in quiet country lanes leading to sleepy market towns and unspoilt villages. To the north rise the intricate folds of the North York Moors: to the south, the Yorkshire Wolds roll gently away towards Beverley, Hull and the River Humber. Our exploration of the vale begins at the eastern end of this broad, low-lying corridor, at East Ayton near Scarborough, and follows it westwards to the lower slopes of the Hambleton Hills.

East Ayton to Pickering

East Ayton   *Map 3 ref J4*
4m E of Scarborough, on the A170

Victorian visitors to Scarborough, occasionally tiring of its urban attractions, welcomed excursions to beauty spots such as the **Forge Valley** near East Ayton. Eons ago, a sharp-edged glacier excavated the valley; then centuries of natural growth softened its hills, clothed them with over-arching trees and, quite by chance, created one of the loveliest woodland walks in England. For a steady walker, going say 4 miles an hour, the round trip walk from East Ayton to the old forge from which the valley derives its name, - along one side of the river returning on the other, takes about 2 1/2 hours. A short diversion will lead you to the ruins of **Ayton Castle** at the edge of the road near the junction of the A170 and B1261. Dating from around 1400, this is one of the most southerly hundreds of pele towers built in those turbulent times as a protection against invading Scottish marauders. In more peaceful days, many of these towers had a more comfortable mansion added but their defensive origins are still clearly recognisable.

On the edge of East Ayton village is a fascinating place that all the family will enjoy visiting called **The Honey Farm**. This outstanding attraction was founded by bee-keeper Steve Ryan and has everything for a great day out. Created only a few years ago, it is now a place that no-one should leave out of a trip to this part of Yorkshire. Visitors can see the bees in their natural surroundings and guided tours help you to learn even more about this fascinating insect. It is the female bees which maintain the home with meticulous care, and the exhibition allows you to see a working colony sited within a tree trunk. Children will love to see the colony established in a doll's house, and even more remarkable is the colonisation of a letter box. It is an incredible fact that in central London about 28 post boxes a day become sites for colonies! Another interesting exhibit is the honey extractor which is used to spin the honey from the combs. Working on a similar principle to a spin dryer, the liquid honey is flung from the cells in the combs by centrifugal force.

One of the most surprising substances to come from a beehive is propolis. Dark brown in colour, propolis is made up of resin from plants and trees, wax, essential oils and pollen. Bees use this to block up cracks in the hive and its antiseptic properties help keep the young bees in a sterile environment. Apparently, propolis has tremendous healing powers and has been used in recent years for blood disorders, ulcers, rashes, coughs and colds, and dental problems as well as to treat some arthritic conditions. Some claim it can even prevent flu.

The Honey Farm

The Honey Farm can boast an outstanding restaurant offering welcome refreshment after a long day sightseeing. It is mainly home cooking that is on offer and there is a bakery on site providing freshly baked vegetables, bread and cakes. The Farm Shop sells cheeses, meat and vegetables, while the craft shops offer the wares of local craftsmen. The Honey Farm Shop sells a variety of honeys, fresh from the hives, and lots of other souvenirs. The shop even stocks an extensive range of cosmetics that incorporate honey and beeswax. A recent addition is a pottery where visitors can watch the talented potter at work and, of course, purchase the results of his labours. This is an unusual and remarkable place, - well worth going out of your way to visit. *The Honey Farm, Betton Farm Centre, East Ayton, nr Scarborough, North Yorkshire, YO13 9HT. Tel: 01723 864001. Tearooms & Farm Shop: Tel: 01723 863143*

Just north of East Ayton, on the edge of the North York Moors National Park, is *East Ayton Lodge*. This beautifully appointed hotel is set in three acres of its own grounds, close to the River Derwent. The tranquil surroundings make this an ideal place for a peaceful and relaxing holiday.

East Ayton Lodge

A well stocked bar caters for all needs, offering a good selection of beers, wines and spirits. Morning coffee is available as well as a large selection of bar meals at lunch time and in the evening. The excellent restaurant specialises in English, French and vegetarian cuisine with fresh vegetables from the hotel garden when in season. You can dine in elegant surroundings and choose from the comprehensive a la carte or table d'hote menus which are complimented by an extensive wine list. There are 31 comfortable bedrooms, all with en suite bathrooms and furnished and equipped to a high standard. There are three honeymoon suites which, together with seven other bedrooms, have four-poster beds, perfect for a romantic break. Whether on business or pleasure, for one night or several, owners Brian and Karry Gardner will make sure you enjoy your stay to the full. *East Ayton Lodge, Moor Lane, East Ayton, Nr. Scarborough, North Yorkshire, YO13 9EW. Tel: 01723 864227 / Fax: 01723 862680*

Ebberston   Map 3 ref I4
11m W of Scarborough, on the A170
Standing in its own grounds, boasting panoramic views across the vale to the Yorkshire Wolds, *Foxholm* is a stone built farmhouse converted into a modern and comfortable Country Hotel. This splendid Hotel has been owned and managed since 1978 by Kay Clyde and offers its guests the best in good old-fashioned British hospitality. All of the comfortable bedrooms are situated on the ground floor

and have full en suite facilities, colour TV, clock radio and complimentary tea and coffee tray.

During 1992 the bar area was extended when the hotel became a fully licensed free house and it has retained much of its old charm, mainly in the wooden carved bar which is covered in old coins. The games room offers a pool table and dart board, and Sky television is available to keep abreast of the sports and news. The cosy residents' lounge has south-facing French doors that lead into the extensive grounds, whilst the pleasant dining room can seat up to twenty guests in comfort. The comprehensive a la carte menu provides a good choice of home cooked dishes which have been prepared using

Foxholm

only the freshest locally-grown seasonal ingredients. Situated in the tranquil village of Ebberston, Foxholm is the perfect place to escape the stresses of everyday life and just sit back and relax. *Foxholm, Ebberston, Nr. Scarborough, North Yorkshire, YO13 9NJ. Tel: 01723 859550*

About a mile to the west of Ebberston, in the early 18th century, Mr William Thompson, MP for Scarborough, built for himself what is possibly the smallest stately home in England, *Ebberston Hall*. From the front, the house appears to be just one storey high, with a pillared doorway approached by a grand flight of stone steps flanked by a moderately sized room on each side. In fact, behind this modest front, there's also an extensive basement - *"deceptively spacious"* as the estate agents say. If you would like to visit Ebberston Hall, please remember that it is open to visitors only by appointment .

Thornton-le-Dale   Map 3 ref H4
14m W of Scarborough, on the A170

As long ago as 1907, a *"Yorkshire Post"* poll of its readers acclaimed Thornton-le-Dale as the most beautiful village in Yorkshire. Despite stiff competition for that title, most visitors find themselves in agreement. If further proof were needed, just off the A170 near the parish church of All Saints, you'll find one of the most photographed houses in Britain, appearing regularly on chocolate boxes, jigsaws and calendars. The North York Moors National Park actually creates a special loop in its boundary to include this picture-postcard village which, somewhat confusingly, is also frequently shown on maps as *"Thornton Dale"*.

Thornton-le-Dale is ideally centred for exploring the wonderful surrounding countryside, the North York Moors and the east coast resorts. On the eastern edge of the village stands *Easthill House*, set in two and a half acres of beautifully laid out grounds and landscaped gardens. This lovely family house has been sympathetically converted to provide three quiet, spacious and very attractive apartments. They accommodate 2-8 people and all enjoy views of the gardens and the Vale of Pickering beyond. An adjoining cottage has been converted from the coachhouse and stable which retains many original features. All the apartments, and the cottage, are self-contained, each with its own private entrance. The furnishings and decor reflect the style of the country house whilst the kitchens are particularly well equipped.

Also to be found in the lovely private grounds of Easthill House are three Scandinavian 'A'-frame chalets known as *Easthill Gardens*, each set in its own clearing, nestling amongst pine trees in a small wooded area. What better place for a peaceful holiday! Care-

Easthill House and Gardens

fully located for privacy, each chalet is tastefully furnished and centrally heated, comprising one twin and one double bedded room, shower room, and large open plan kitchen / dining/sitting area with a verandah giving views over open countryside.

Easthill House and Gardens also offers a grass tennis court, a putting green, adventure play area and a small indoor games area. Ample car parking. Sorry - no pets. *Easthill House & Gardens, Thornton-le-Dale, North Yorkshire, YO18 7QP. Tel: 01751 474561*

Pickering

This busy little town developed around the important crossroads where the Malton to Whitby, and the Thirsk to Scarborough roads intersect. It's the largest of the four market towns in Ryedale and possibly the oldest, claiming to date from 270 BC when (so it's said) it was founded by a King of the Brigantes called Peredurus. William the Conqueror's attempts to dominate the area are recalled by Pickering's ruined castle, and the many inns and posting houses reflect the town's prosperity during the stage coach era. Lying at the heart of the fertile Vale of Pickering, the town's reputation was originally based on its famous pigs and horses. Vast quantities of pork were transported across the moors to Whitby, salted and used as ship-board rations. The famous Cleveland Bay horses, with their jet-black manes and tails, were extensively bred in the area. (In Eskdale, a little further north, they still are). These sweet-natured, sturdy and tireless animals have always been in great demand. During the 19th century, their equable temperament made them ideal for pulling Hansom cabs and street-cars, and nowadays they are often seen in more dignified events such as State Processions.

The parish church of **St Peter and St Paul** is well worth visiting for its remarkable 15th century murals. During the glum days of Puritanism, these lively paintings were denounced as idolatrous and plastered over. They stayed forgotten for some two hundred years but were re-discovered when the church was being restored in 1851. Unfortunately, the vicar at that time shared the Puritans' sentiments and, despite opposition from his parishioners and even from his bishop, had them smothered again under whitewash. A more liberal successor to the Vicar had the murals restored once again in 1878 and they now give one a vivid idea of how cheerful, colourful and entertaining many English churches were before the unforgivable vandalism of the Puritan years. These superb paintings, sharp, vigorous and well-observed, happily embrace scenes from the Bible, old legends and actual history: a real insight into the medieval mind that had no difficulty in accepting both the story of St George slaying the dragon and the martyrdom of St Thomas a Becket as equally real, and inspiring, events.

Also not to be missed in Pickering is the **Beck Isle Museum** housed in a gracious Regency mansion. Its 27 display areas are crammed with a *"magnificent assortment of items curious, mysterious, marvellous and commonplace from the last 200 years"*. There are intriguing re-creations of typical Victorian domestic rooms, shops, workshops and even a pub. The comprehensive collection of photographs by Sydney Smith presents a remarkable picture of the Ryedale area as it was more than half a century ago. The exhibition is made even more interesting by its acquisition of the very cameras and other photographic equipment used by Sydney Smith.

If you catch a whiff of sulphurous smoke, then you must be close to the station. Pickering is the southern terminus of the **North York Moors Railway** and here you can board a steam-drawn train for an 18-mile journey along one of the oldest and most dramatically scenic railways in the country. And at the **Pickering Trout Lake** you can hire a rod and tackle and attempt to beat the record for the largest fish caught here - it currently stands at a mighty 25lb 4oz (11.45 kg).

Pickering to Malton

Kirby Misperton   *Map 2 ref H5*
5m S of Pickering, off the A169
A few miles south of Pickering, the 375 acres of wooded parkland surrounding Kirby Misperton Hall provide an attractive setting for **Flamingo Land,** a Zoo and Fun Park that is home to more than 1,000 birds, animals and reptiles. Beyond doubt, the most spectacular sight is that of the flock of pink flamingoes gathered around the lake fringed with willow trees. With more than one hundred different attractions, including a fun fair, an adventure playground and a real working farm, this is an ideal venue for families with young children.

Situated to the east of Kirby Misperton, just off the A169 Pickering to Malton road, you will find the **Bean Sheaf Hotel and Restaurant**. The hotel is spacious, comfortable and modern, complementing the original restaurant, parts of which date back to the 17th century. There are 20 en suite bedrooms available, all furnished

The Bean Sheaf Hotel & Restaurant

and equipped to a luxurious standard. There are double, twin and family rooms, a special four-poster suite for special occasions, and two specially designed rooms for the disabled. The hotel features a sauna, and is set within 2 acres of grounds with attractive gardens and a fish pond. Attached to the hotel, so that guests have no need to go outside, is the Bean Sheaf Restaurant. Run by Liz and Michele Sardone, who also run the hotel, here Michele reigns supreme. Having trained in Switzerland, he is an outstanding chef offering English and Continental cuisine of a high standard. The menus are wide ranging and reasonably priced, and all dishes feature the best of fresh local produce and vegetables from the hotel garden. You can be assured of a warm welcome, and you are guaranteed to enjoy your visit. E.T.B. 3-Crowns Commended. *The Bean Sheaf Hotel & Restaurant, Kirby Misperton, nr Pickering, North Yorkshire, YO17 0UE Tel: 01653 668614 / 668488. Fax: 01653 668370*

Malton
Map 2 ref H6

8m S of Pickering, off the A169/B1257

Malton has been the historic centre of Ryedale ever since the Romans came. They built a large fort and called it *"Derventio"* after the river Derwent beside which it stands. For many years, archaeologists were puzzled by the large scale of the fort, a mystery resolved in 1970 when a building dedication was uncovered which revealed that the fort housed a cavalry regiment, the *"Ala*

Picentiana", - the extra space was needed to accommodate their horses. Many relics from the site, showing the sophisticated life-styles of the Roman centurions and civilians, can be seen in the **Malton Museum,** along with items from the Iron Age settlement that preceded the Roman garrison.

The River Derwent was vitally important to Malton. The river rises in the moors near Scarborough, then runs inland through the Vale of Pickering bringing an essential element for what was once a major industry in Malton - brewing. In the 19th century, there were nine breweries here, now only the **Malton Brewery Company** survives. It operates in a converted stable block behind Suddabys Crown Hotel in Wheelgate and welcomes visitors, but telephone them first on 01653 697580.

In December each year, Malton hosts a colourful Dickensian Festival. Charles Dickens stayed nearby with his friend, Charles Smithson, a solicitor, and is believed to have modelled Scrooge's Counting House in *"A Christmas Carol"* on Smithson's office in Chancery Lane.

Just to the north of Malton is **Eden Camp**, a theme museum dedicated to re-creating the dramatic experiences of ordinary people living through World War II. This unique museum is housed in the huts of a genuine prisoner of war camp, built in 1942. Sound, lighting effects, smells, even smoke generators are deployed to make you feel that you are actually there, taking part. Visitors can find out what it was like to live through an air raid, to be a prisoner of war or a sailor in a U-boat under attack. Amongst the many other exhibits are displays on Fashion in the 40s, Children at War, and even one on Rationing - in 1941, one discovers, the cheese ration was down to 1oz a week!

Right next door to Eden Camp is **Eden Farm Insight,** a working farm with a fascinating collection of old farm machinery and implements, (including a very old horse wheel), lots of animals, a blacksmith's and a wheelwright's shop, as well as a choice of farm walks, all clearly signposted and with useful information boards. The Farm also offers a cafe, gift shop, and a picnic and play area.

Old Malton
Map 2 ref H5

1 mile N of Malton off the A64

Old Malton is located just to the north of the Roman Fort, an interesting and historic area on the edge of open countryside. Nearby villages such as Settrington and their secluded country lanes are home to many famous racehorse stables: if you are up and about early enough you will see the horses out on their daily exercises.

The **Wentworth Arms** in Old Malton is an ideal centre from which you could take in this morning ritual and also provides the perfect location for many other attractions and activities in the region. The Moors, the Dales, the Wolds and the east coast resorts are all easily reached. The City of York is less than twenty miles away and many picturesque villages wait to be explored.

The Wentworth Arms was originally a coaching inn with its history stretching back to the early 1700s. For over one hundred years, it has been in the same family: Mr and Mrs Smith, the present licensees, are the fourth generation. Over the years, the Wentworth has undergone modernization and refurbishment. The present dining room, which was at one time a barn, has retained its old world atmosphere with original beams and stone walls.

The Wentworth Arms

The hotel is fully centrally heated with the additional warmth of log fires in the bar and lounge on cooler days. The guest bedrooms are comfortably furnished and most have en suite facilities. The modern beds have electric blankets, and television and hot drinks facilities are in all rooms. Good quality food can be enjoyed at all meal times in the restaurant and bar areas. English Tourist Board approved. *The Wentworth Arms, Old Malton, Malton, North Yorkshire, YO17 0HD. Tel: 01653 692618*

In the centre of Old Malton stands a beautiful fragment of **St Mary's Priory** with a particularly fine Norman doorway. The Priory was built around 1155 by the only monastic order in Christendom to have originated entirely in England, - the Gilbertines. The order was founded in 1148 by a Lincolnshire parish priest, St Gilbert of Sempringham.

Parts of the parish church are quite as old as the Priory but one of its most interesting features is relatively modern, the work of the 'Mouseman of Kilburn', Robert Thompson. A gifted woodcarver and furniture maker, Thompson 'signed' all his pieces with a discreetly placed carving of a mouse. There's one on the stout oak door of the church and, inside, the stalls are carved elaborately with all manner of wondrous beasts and historical and mythical scenes.

Malton to Helmsley

Welburn   Map 2 ref G6
5m SW of Malton, off the A64
About 5 miles west of Malton, lying in the folds of the Howardian Hills, stands one of the most glorious stately homes in Britain, ***Castle Howard***. Well known to television viewers as the Brideshead of *"Brideshead Revisited"*, Castle Howard has astonished visitors ever since it was completed in the early 1700s. Even that world-weary 18th century socialite Horace Walpole was stirred to enthusiasm: *"Nobody had informed me"* he wrote *"that at one view I should see a palace, a town, a fortified city, temples on high places,...the noblest lawn in the world fenced by half the horizon and a mausoleum that would tempt one to be buried alive: in short, I have seen gigantic places before, but never a sublime one".* Perhaps the most astonishing fact of all concerns the architect of Castle Howard, Sir John

Castle Howard

Vanbrugh. Vanbrugh had been a soldier and a playwright but until he began this sublime building had never yet overseen the placing of one block of masonry on another.

A grand tree-lined avenue, four miles long, leads to Castle Howard. Near the southern end of this impressive approach lies the village of Welburn and on its main street the **Crown and Cushion** pub, a charming late 18th century establishment which, as far as anyone can tell, has always had this unusual name. The pub is run by Maggie and John Tate-Smith who, although having been here less than a year, have years of experience in the trade.

Crown and Cushion

A charming inn, the interior is decorated and furnished in a style in keeping with the age of the building and is a wonderful atmosphere in which to enjoy a pint or two of the excellent beers and ales that are on offer. That, however, is not all because, when they arrived here, Maggie and John also brought with them a wonderful lady chef, Sam, who creates a whole host of tasty and delicious meals for visitors at both lunchtime and in the evening. A popular place, it is advisable to book a table in the cosy restaurant to avoid disappointment. When planning a visit to the pub, remember that it is closed on Monday lunchtimes and no meals on served on Monday evenings, except on Bank Holidays. Otherwise, this is a wonderful place to come to both during the winter when it is warm and cosy inside, and in the summer when the attractive beer garden is a riot of colour. *Crown and Cushion, Welburn, North Yorkshire, YO6 7DZ. Tel: 01653 618304*

Two miles south of Welburn, in a lovely, peaceful setting beside the River Derwent, stand the remains of ***Kirkham Priory***. According to legend, the priory was founded in 1125 by Walter l'Espec after his only son was thrown from his horse and killed at this very spot. (A few years later, Walter was to found another great abbey at

Kirkham Priory

Rievaulx). Visitors to Kirkham pass through a noble, exquisitely decorated gatehouse but one of the most memorable sights at the Priory, perhaps because it is so unexpected, is the sumptuous lavatorium in the ruined cloister. Here the monks washed their hands at two bays with lavishly moulded arches supported by slender pillars, each bay adorned with tracery.

Sinnington
Map 2 ref G4

4m W of Pickering, off the A170

At Sinnington the River Seven leaves the moors and the valley of Rosedale for the more open country of the Vale. It passes through this tiny village, running alongside a broad green in the centre of which is a graceful old packhorse bridge. At one time this medieval bridge must have served a useful purpose but the old watercourse that ran beneath it is now dry.

Here, set amidst beautiful scenery and ideal for those who enjoy walking and the peace of the countryside, is the *Fox and Hounds*. It's a wonderful example of a true country retreat yet only 400 yards from the main road. Back in the 18th century it was a thriving coaching inn on the main route from the east coast to Thirsk and points west.

The Fox and Hounds

A welcoming richness of antiques, ancient wood panelling and oak beams greet you on arrival. The owners, Andrew and Catherine Stephens, and their courteous, well-trained staff offer a friendly welcome and a relaxing atmosphere. A choice of ground floor or first-floor accommodation is available from the ten comfortable en suite bedrooms. The restaurant has a full a la carte menu which offers a comprehensive selection of imaginative dishes, all cooked to order. Meals are available in the bar and brasserie. Special midweek and weekend breaks are available. E.T.B. - 4 Crowns Highly Commended. *Fox and Hounds, Main Street, Sinnington, York, YO6 6SQ Tel: 01751 431577*

Kirkbymoorside
Map 2 ref G4

7m W of Pickering, off the A170

Set quietly off the main road, this agreeable market town of fine Georgian houses, narrow twisting lanes and cobbled market place, straggles up the hillside. Where the town ends, the moors begin.

In the heart of this picturesque little town, and just a quarter of a mile from the main road, is the *George and Dragon Hotel*. Since

The George & Dragon Hotel

the 1600s, this has been a coaching inn, a natural stopping place on the Great North Road providing a haven of warmth, refreshment, good cheer and rest. Today, the hospitality is just as good, especially from owners Stephen and Frances Colling. The food has an excellent reputation with a wide range of meals always on offer. There are three fully qualified chefs employed and their handiwork can be sampled in the bar and the candlelit restaurant. The hotel has recently been awarded an AA Rosette for its outstanding cuisine. Behind the bar there is always a good range of real ales available, and since Stephen has a background as a wine merchant his wine list features carefully chosen and interesting wines. The decor has a sporting theme throughout, and the George and Dragon frequently holds dinners hosted by sporting personalities. To the rear are a converted corn mill and rectory which now house 19 bedrooms. All the rooms have en suite facilities and one has a feature four-poster bed. Most enjoy the benefit of views over the pretty walled garden. E.T.B. 4-Crowns Commended. *George and Dragon Hotel, Market Place, Kirkbymoorside, North Yorkshire, YO6 6AA. Tel / Fax: 01751 433334*

Facing the attractive Market Square in the centre of Kirkbymoorside stands **The White Swan**. Dating back to the 1600s, this delightful Inn is packed with olde worlde charm and character, with original oak beams, large open fireplaces and plenty of horse brasses glowing in the firelight. Before the 1960s the pub had three main rooms but these were opened up into one large main room which allows visitors to move about freely. Ian Major, your resident

The White Swan

host, bought the pub back in 1995 and has prided himself on serving only the best traditional ales, including Tetley's, Black Sheep and numerous guest ales. The White Swan has already been featured in the Camra Good Beer Guide for 1998 and hopes to win plenty more awards for its excellent beer. With darts, pool and dominoes always available, and a large beer garden to the rear of the Inn, we are sure that visitors to this traditional pub will always find something to interest and amuse them. *The White Swan, 4 Church Street, Kirkbymoorside, North Yorkshire, YO6 6AZ. Tel: 01751 431441*

The King's Head Hotel, a former 17th century coaching inn, can be found on the main road through the town. In the past, stage coaches would have rumbled through what is now the entrance hall and a bell, which now hangs in the bar, would have been rung to summon passengers to the coach. The 2nd Duke of Buckingham, the notorious George Villiers, is said to have died at adjoining Buckingham House, once part of the King's Head Hotel. The Duke, once a bosom companion of Charles II, had squandered a vast fortune and by the 1680s was reduced to living in some squalor at Helmsley Castle. While hunting on the moors near Kirkbymoorside, the Duke's horse dropped dead under him. While waiting for a new mount, he caught a severe chill and was carried to the King's Head. Before dying, the Duke was able to write a last latter which contains a

The King's Head Hotel

typically sardonic adieu: *"The world and I shake hands, for I dare affirm we are heartily weary of each other"*. His passing was recorded in the parish register with a laconic entry reading, *"April 17th George Viluas: Lord Dooke of Bookingham"*.

Today the hotel is run by the Riby family - Sheila, Tony and their daughter Louise. There are two bar areas to choose from. The Duke's Bar features the original flagstone floors and a log fire, while the Hiker's Bar in the brewhouse offers pool and darts for the young at heart. The distinctive and eye-catching restaurant area can seat up to 40 and offers freshly prepared and home-cooked food. The varied menu is accompanied by daily specials listed on a blackboard. There is accommodation available with nine letting rooms, four of which have en suite facilities. The breakfasts are highly recommended and, as they are large, extra time should be allowed to finish them! *The King's Head Hotel, High Market Place, Kirkbymoorside, North Yorkshire, YO6 6AT. Tel: 01751 431340*

Helmsley
Map 2 ref F4

13m E of Thirsk, on the A170

One of North Yorkshire's most popular and attractive towns, Helmsley lies on the banks of the River Rye at the edge of the North York Moors National Park. The spacious market square is typical of the area but the Gothic memorial to the 2nd Earl of Feversham that stands there is not. This astonishingly ornate construction was designed by Sir Giles Gilbert Scott and looks like a smaller version of his famous memorial to Sir Walter Scott in Edinburgh.

The Earls of Feversham lived at **Duncombe Park** whose extensive grounds sweep up to within a few yards of the Market Place. Most of the original mansion, designed by Vanbrugh, was gutted by a disastrous fire in 1879: only the north wing remained habitable and that in its turn was ruined by a second fire in 1895. The Fevershams lavished a fortune on rebuilding the grand old house, largely to the original design, but the financial burden eventually forced them to lease the house and grounds as a preparatory school for girls. Happily, the Feversham were able to return to their ancestral home in 1985 and the beautifully restored house and lovely grounds are now open to the public.

Before they were ennobled, the Fevershams family name was Duncombe and it was Sir Thomas Duncombe, a wealthy London goldsmith, who established the family seat here when he bought **Helmsley Castle** (English Heritage) and its estate in 1687. Founded in the early 1100s, seriously knocked about during the Civil War, the castle was in a dilapidated state but its previous owner, the Duke of Buckingham, had continued to live there in some squalor and discomfort. Sir Thomas quickly decided to build a more suitable residence nearby, abandoning the ruins to lovers of the romantic and picturesque.

Helmsley Castle

Sitting on the market square in Helmsley, the **Royal Oak** is as attractive inside as it is outside. Formerly a coaching inn and posting house, the inn was rebuilt in 1896. In 1994, it was taken over by

Duncombe Park

The Royal Oak

Camerons Brewery who, along with recent new managers Dave and Suzy Peters, are successfully building on its long-standing reputation for delicious food, excellent ale and outstanding accommodation.

The interior is Victorian and, as well as being excellently decorated and furnished, there are some unusual ornaments and memorabilia to be admired. The Royal Oak can boast five letting rooms which are truly luxurious. Each room has en suite facilities, some feature four-poster beds, and all are spacious and comfortable. The food available is of an equally good quality. The menu offers a good selection with extra daily specials detailed on the blackboard and all dishes are good value for money. Behind the bar, there is a fine array of well-kept real ales and, of course, the usual selection of beers and spirits. Food is served Monday to Saturday from 12 noon - 2pm and 5.30 - 8.30pm, and on Sundays from 12 noon until 2pm.
The Royal Oak, Market Place, Helmsley, North Yorkshire, YO6 5BL Tel: 01439 770450

Church Farm Holidays, based in Helmsley, offer a superb selection of well-equipped, smartly furnished accommodation. Each of the cottages and apartments has been newly-built using traditional local stone and have been designed to form a quiet courtyard. The self-catering accommodation ranges from a flat for two people to a cottage which can sleep up to six.

Church Farm has also been the home to the Otterburn family for generations. Although it is no longer a working farm, Christine and

Rievaulx Abbey

Richard Otterburn now run a thriving home made ice cream business called ***The Ryeburn Ice Cream Parlour*** from buildings which have been carefully converted and sympathetically constructed. It's well worth popping in here to spoil yourself with one of the many special award-winning concoctions. All the ice cream and other products, including fudge, are made in the factory and are on sale. David,

**Church Farm Holidays and Ryeburn
Ice Cream Parlour**

the ice cream maker, has won over 20 diplomas for his ice cream. The dairy is open to the public as well, so they can see the ice cream and sorbets being processed. There is also a cafe selling refreshments and snacks. *Church Farm Holidays and Ryeburn Ice Cream Parlour, Church Farm, Cleveland Way, Helmsley, North Yorkshire, YO6 5AE. Tel: 01439 770331*

Rievaulx
Map 2 ref E4

2 miles W of Helmsley off the B1257

Just to the west of Helmsley rise the indescribably beautiful remains of **Rievaulx Abbey** (English Heritage), standing amongst wooded hills beside the River Rye, - *"the most beautiful monastic site in Europe"*. JMW Turner was enchanted by this idyllic landscape; Dorothy Wordsworth, 'spellbound'. Founded in 1131, it was the first Cistercian abbey in Yorkshire and, with some 700 people -

monks, lay brothers, servants -eventually living within its walls, became one of the largest. Like Kirkham Abbey a few years earlier, Rievaulx was endowed by Walter l'Espec, Lord of Helmsley, still mourning the loss of his only son in a riding accident. The Abbey was soon a major landowner in the county, earning a healthy income from farming - at one time owning more than 14,000 sheep. The Abbey also had its own fishery at Teesmouth, and iron-ore mines at Bilsdale and near Wakefield.

Looking down on the extensive remains of the Abbey is ***Rievaulx Terrace*** (National Trust), a breathtaking example of landscape gardening completed in 1758. The cunningly contrived avenues draw your eyes to incomparable views of the Abbey itself, to vistas along the Rye Valley and to the rolling contours of the hills beyond. At each end of the terrace is a classical temple, one of which is elaborately decorated as a dining room.

Hawnby   Map 2 ref E4
5 miles NW of Helmsley off the B1257

A few miles north of Rievaulx lies Easterside Farm, a real hidden gem; surrounded by thousands of acres of unspoilt countryside and with breathtaking views in all directions it lies just outside the village of Hawnby. Built in the mid-18th century, the farmhouse has been the home of Sarah and Alan Wood since 1990 and they have been offering wonderful bed and breakfast accommodation for most of their time here. There are three guest bedrooms, all en-suite, in the main farmhouse and two more in a recently converted farm building that used to house the granary and cart shed. All are com-

Easterside Farm

fortable, full of character and charm, as well as catering for the needs of a family on holiday.

Ideal for children, they can play safely outside in the farmhouse garden whilst parents can keep an eye on them from the patio. A true home from home, Sarah and Alan aim to make everyone's stay here a holiday to remember and can provide evening meals by prior arrangement as well as offer packed lunches on request. *Easterside Farm, Hawnby, Nr. Helmsley, North Yorkshire YO6 5QT Tel: 01439 798277*

Harome   Map 2 ref F5
2 miles SE of Helmsley off the A170

On a minor road, two and a half miles southeast of Helmsley, you will come to the charming village of Harome where, in a superb position overlooking the village pond, is the extremely well-appointed **Pheasant Hotel**. This splendidly renovated and extended country hotel occupies the former village blacksmith's workshop, a shop, and two cottages. Today it has twelve bedrooms, all with private bathroom, colour televisions, and tea/coffee making facilities, as well as two self-contained suites and two attractive cottages which are run

The Pheasant Hotel

as a fully-serviced part of the hotel. A large garden and paddock provide fresh produce for the hotel kitchen where the preparation of the finest English food is supervised by the owner, Mrs Tricia Binks. The hotel has a heated indoor swimming pool. Unfortunately, credit cards cannot be accepted. *The Pheasant Hotel, Harome, Helmsley, North Yorkshire, YO6 5JG. Tel: 01439 71241 / 70416*

Nunnington Hall (National Trust), about four miles southeast of Harome, is a late 17th century manor house set beside the River

Rye with a picturesque packhorse bridge within its grounds. Inside, there is a magnificent panelled hall, fine tapestries and china, and the famous Carlisle collection of miniature rooms exquisitely furnished in different period styles to one eighth life size.

CHAPTER FIVE
In & Around York

York Minster

Chapter 5 - Area Covered

For precise location of places please refer to the colour maps found at the rear of the book.

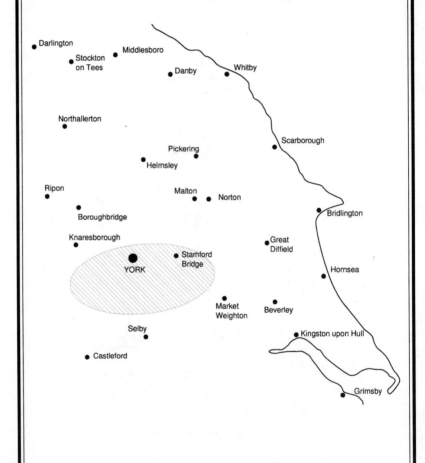

5
In & Around York

York

"The history of York is the history of England" said the Duke of York, later to become George VI. A bold claim but well justified. For almost two thousand years the city has been at the centre of great events and, better than any other city in England, it has preserved the evidence of its glorious past. One of the grandest cityscapes in the country opens up as you walk along the old city walls towards **York Minster,** a sublime expression of medieval faith.

The Minster stands on the site of an even older building, the headquarters of the Roman legions. The Imperial troops arrived here in AD71 when the governor, Quintus Petilius Cerealis, chose this strategic position astride the Rivers Ouse and Foss as his base for a campaign against the pesky tribe of the Brigantes. The settlement was named Eboracum. From this garrison, Hadrian directed the construction of his great wall and a later general, Constantine, was proclaimed Emperor here. The legions finally left the city around AD410, but the evidence of their three and a half centuries of occupation is manifest all around York in buildings like the **Multangular Tower,** in rich artefacts treasured in the city's museums and even in a pub: at the **Roman Bath Inn** you can see the remains of steam baths used by the garrison residents.

Little is known of York during the Dark Ages but by the 8th century the city had been colonised by the Anglo-Saxons, who named it *"Eoferwic,"* and it was already an important Christian and academic centre. The Vikings put an end to that when they invaded in the 9th century and changed the name once again, this time to Jorvik. The story of York during those years of Danish rule is imaginatively told in the many displays at the ***Jorvik Centre***.

After the Norman Conquest, the city suffered badly during the Harrowing of the North when William the Conqueror mounted a brutal campaign against his rebellious northern subjects. Vast tracts of Yorkshire and Northumberland were laid waste and some historians reckon that it took more than a hundred years for the area to recover from this wholesale devastation.

In later Norman times, however, York entered one of its most glorious periods. The Minster, the largest Gothic church in England, was begun around 1230 and the work was on such a scale that it would not be completed until two and a half centuries later. Its stained glass windows - there are more than a hundred of them - cast an celestial light over the many treasures within. A guided tour of the Great Tower gives dizzying views across the city; a visit to the crypt reveals some of the relics from the Roman fortress that stood here nearly 2000 years ago.

Clifford's Tower, York

This superb building has survived seemingly unscathed from three major fires. The first occurred in 1829 and was started by a madman, Jonathan Martin. Believing that God wanted him to destroy the church, he started a fire using prayer and hymn books. The fire not discovered until the following morning by which time the east end of the Minster had been severely damaged. The second blaze, in 1840, was caused by a workman leaving a candle burning. As a result of his carelessness, the central part of the nave was destroyed.

The most recent conflagration was in July 1984, shortly after a controversial Bishop of Durham had been installed. Some attributed the fire to God's wrath at the Bishop's appointment; the more prosaic view was that it had been caused by lightning. The subsequent restoration has allowed modern masons and craftsmen to demonstrate that they possess skills just as impressive as those of their medieval forebears.

The network of medieval streets around the Minster is one of the city's major delights. Narrow lanes are criss-crossed by even narrower footpaths - ginnels, snickets or *"snickelways"*, which have survived as public rights of way despite being built over, above and around. Narrowest of all the snickelways is Pope's Head Alley, more than 100ft long but only 31 inches wide. The alley was also known as Introduction Lane, - if you wanted to know someone better, you simply timed your walk along it so as to meet the other party halfway. Whip-ma-Whop-ma-Gate, allegedly, is where felons used to be *"whipped and whopped"*. Probably most famous of these ancient streets is **The Shambles**. Its name comes from *"Fleshammels"*, the street of butchers and slaughter houses. The houses here were deliberately built to keep the street out of direct sunlight, thus protecting the carcasses which were hung outside the houses on hooks. Many of the hooks are still in place.

During these years, York was the second largest city in England and it was then that the town walls and their 'bars', or gates, were built. The trade guilds were also at their most powerful and in Fossgate one of them built the lovely black and white timbered **Merchant Adventurers Hall**. The Merchant Adventurers controlled the lucrative trade in all "goods bought and sold foreign" and they spared no expense in building their Great Hall where they conducted their affairs benath a complex timbered roof displaying many colourful banners of York's medieval guilds. To this period too belong the **York Mystery Plays**, first performed in 1397 and subsequently every four years.

During Tudor times, York's importance steadily declined but reemerged in the 18th century as a fashionable social centre. Many elegant Georgian houses, of which **Fairfax House** in Castlegate is perhaps the most splendid, were built at this time and they add another attractive architectural dimension to the city.

The following century saw York take on a completely different role as the hub of the railway system in the north. At the heart of this transformation was the charismatic entrepreneur George Hudson, founder of what became the Great Northern Railway, part visionary, part crook. His wheeler-dealing eventually led to his disgrace but even then the citizens of York twice elected him as Lord Mayor and he still has a pub named after him. It was thanks to Hudson that York's magnificent railway station, with its great curving roof of glass, was built, a tourist attraction in its own right. Nearby, in Leeman Street, is the **National Railway Museum**, the largest of its kind in the world. This fascinating exhibition covers some two hundred years of railway history, from **Stephenson's Rocket** to the Channel Tunnel. Amongst the thousands of exhibits demonstrating the technical and social impact of the *"Iron Horse"* are Gresley's record-breaking locomotive, Mallard, Queen Victoria's royal carriage, and displays demonstrating the workings of the railway system. There's an extensive library and reading room (booking advised), and the *"Brief Encounter"* restaurant is themed on the classic movie.

Another aspect of railway history is on view at the **York Model Railway**, next door to the station, which has almost one third of a mile of track and up to 14 trains running at any one time. Machinery of a very different kind is on display at the **Museum of Automata**. Automata are *"man made objects that imitate the movement of living things through a mechanism that is concealed, so as to make them appear to move spontaneously"*. The museum traces the history of automata, from the simple articulated figurines of ancient civilisations, through to displays of modern robotics: the Automata Shop sells contemporary pieces, music boxes, mechanical

The Royal Oak

toys and craft kits suitable for all ages.

It's impossible here to list all York's museums, galleries and fine buildings, but you will find a wealth of additional information at the Tourist Information Centre close to one of the historic old gateways to the city, ***Bootham Bar.***

In Goodramgate is ***The Royal Oak***. It can only be described as a unique old inn, with its traditional, cosy, welcoming atmosphere and excellent home cooked fayre which makes any visitor want to return time after time. The Royal Oak has won awards for catering excellence, which is not surprising as the menus are distinctly creative, with not a chip of French fry to be seen! All the food is cooked on the premises, including the delicious bread buns. Meals are plentiful, representing superb value and served from 11am - 8pm daily. The beers are hand-pulled traditional ales of a consistently high standard and, to confirm this, The Royal Oak has been selected by CAMRA for entry into the Good Beer guide for the past 20 years - an achievement accomplished by very few! There are three separate rooms, one of which is set aside for non-smoking families. The pub also features murals by a local artist, Jenny Hill. *The Royal Oak, Goodramgate, York, YO1 2LG. Tel: 01904 653856*

For a taste of traditional English food at its best, then pay a visit to one of ***Russell's Restaurants***. Both are housed in historic listed buildings, conveniently situated in the heart of the city and ideal for that special treat while shopping or sight-seeing. Choose either the Victorian elegance of Russell's of Stonegate, in York's most picturesque street leading to the Minster, or enjoy the rustic atmosphere of Russell's of Coppergate, a 16th century timbered building, formerly a coaching inn.

Russell's Restaurant, Coppergate

Russell's Restaurant, Stonegate

After a warm personal welcome from the friendly staff, guests can relax in style and savour the pleasure of the Russell's experience - quality food, wine and service offering true value for money at affordable prices. First choose from a wide selection of appetising, freshly prepared starters. Then the highlight of the meal is a visit to the carving table for succulent roasts and other main dishes, with fresh local vegetables and cool, refreshing salads. All will definitely be spoilt for choice! For dessert, try their famous bread and butter pudding, or any other from the tempting array of home made sweets. Finally, for the perfect ending, there are Russell's speciality liqueur coffees. Russell's Restaurants are open all day serving coffees, lunches, afternoon teas and evening dinners. *Russell's Restaurants, 34 Stonegate, York, YO1 2AS. Tel: 01904 641432*

A few axe-lengths from the Russell's Restaurant in Coppergate is the **Jorvik Centre**, a fairly recent innovation celebrating a 1000 year old story. Visitors step aboard a time-car for a journey through representations of real-life Viking Age Britain. You pass through a bustling market thronged with Danes bartering for chickens, corn and other provisions and wares, penetrate dark smoky houses, cross a busy wharf where goods transported along the rivers Ouse and Foss are being off-loaded. The experience comes complete with authentic sounds and even smells and for children in particular is both fun and educational.

Jorvik Centre

Situated down a quiet residential street, within five minutes stroll of the city centre, is **The Bronte Guest House**. With a friendly and informal atmosphere, this small family-run business offers guests a comfortable and relaxing place from which to enjoy the delights of medieval York. Most of the bedrooms are en suite and offer all the comforts of larger establishments: the two bedrooms not en suite have use of the house bathroom. Guests have access to the rooms at all times and there is also a guest lounge for catching up on the day's exploration and meeting other guests. Whilst providing all the above, the charming hosts, Yvonne and David, also offer a wide choice for breakfast, from light warm croissants, fruit and yoghurts, to a full English cooked breakfast. Lashings of tea and coffee help wash down the meal and vegetarian and special diets are catered for with advance notice. There cannot be many better places to bring the family than the Bronte Guest House which, whilst overlooking some of the famous sights of York, has also recently won the York Child Friendly Award. *The Bronte Guest House, 22 Grosvenor Terrace, Bootham, York, YO3 7AG. Tel: 01904 621066*

The Bronte Guest House

In a beautifully restored church close to the Shambles is the **Archaeological Research Centre** (ARC), an award-winning hands-on exploration of archaeology for visitors of all ages. Here you can meet practising archaeologists who will demonstrate how to sort and identify genuine finds or to try out ancient crafts. For the more technically minded, there's a series of interactive computer displays which illustrate how modern technology helps to discover and interpret the past. Fascinating.

Very popular with those who have an interest in the more macabre aspects of York's long history is the **Original Ghostwalk of York** which starts at the King's Arms pub on Ouse Bridge and sets off at 8pm every evening. At the last count, York was reckoned to have some 140 resident ghosts within its walls - on this guided walk you visit some of their haunts and hear dark tales, grim accounts of murder, torture, and intrigue. Prepare to have your blood chilled.

The Bar Convent, found in an elegant Georgian building on the western side of the city centre, is an unusual and interesting place to visit. Much more than just a museum and gallery, this is a place where history lives. In the 17th century, a Yorkshire woman called Mary Ward decided to dedicate her life to God but not to the enclosed life of a nun. The Order she founded, the Institute of the Blessed Virgin Mary, set up schools for girls throughout Europe and the members of the Institute are still active today. After Mary's death in 1645, one of her order, Mother Frances Bedingfield, was given money to purchase a house in York and this she did in 1686.

The Order lived at the Bar Convent discreetly, as this was a time of Catholic repression in Britain when the practising and teaching of their faith was outlawed. The Convent's neo-classical chapel, completed in 1769, has nine exits which provided escape routes for the congregation in the event of a raid by the local magistrates, and the dome was completely hidden from the outside. The beautiful chapel is still in use today and a weekly Mass is held.

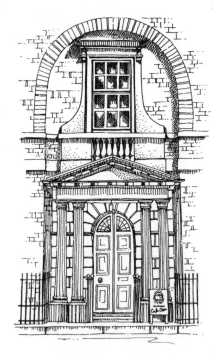

The Bar Convent's Museum tells the story of the Institute of the Blessed Virgin Mary, the pioneering work of the founder and her followers in the area of women's education, and the early history of Christianity in the north of England. The tradition of teaching is continued by the sisters today and, as well as organising group activities, the Bar Convent Heritage project ensures that this Institute has become a place for detailed research.

For the casual visitor, the Museum and chapel make a very interesting visit, but there

The Bar Convent

is a lot more here besides: the wonderful glazed courtyard, the shop selling a wide range of cards, books, posters and religious artefacts, the cafe serving light refreshments to the public as well as Museum visitors, and there is also comfortable accommodation for 22 overnight guests. *The Bar Convent, 17 Blossom Street, York, YO2 2AH. Tel: 01904 643238*

The Maltings public house, in the heart of the city, has been licensed since 1842 and it is York's premier cask ale pub. Highly praised by CAMRA, The Maltings prides itself on the number of

The Maltings

real ales it offers and over a three month period there are some 250 to choose from. Most beers and ales are obtained from smaller, independent breweries and, as might be expected, this establishment is a must for anyone who enjoys a good pint. Visitors can also, if here between noon and 2pm (or until 4pm on Sundays) enjoy a tasty light meal from the pub's imaginative menu. With the interesting array of signs which decorate the walls of the pub, and the warm and friendly atmosphere, this is a super place to come to for a real pint and some pleasant company. *The Maltings, Tanner's Moat, York, YO1 1HU. Tel: 01904 655387*

Around York

In this section we visit some of the villages lying in the Vale of York. The Vale, or Plain as it's sometimes called, is rich, agricultural land that stretches some 60 miles northwards almost to the Tees. Although flat itself, there are almost always hills in view: the Hambleton and Cleveland Hills to the east, the Dales and the Pennines to the west. Parts of it are described in other chapters, the locations mentioned here are all within a few miles of York itself.

Acomb   *Map 4 ref E7*
On the western edge of York, off the B1224

The Sun Inn, situated opposite the village green, dates back to the early 1800s when it was a coaching inn and teams of horses were kept here so that they could be changed on the carriage's way to York - now only a ten minute car journey away. The main bar has an interesting array of pictures of Matt Busby and some of the great Manchester United players as well as well-known jockeys. In the lounge there is a rather fine collection of tea-pots and other items of

The Sun Inn

crockery on display. Though The Sun Inn does not serve food, it does serve an excellent pint of real ale including North Yorkshire's very own Black Sheep. Expertly run by landlady Maureen Yoward with the help of her son John, this is a true English pub and, as such, guests can be sure of a warm welcome. Traditional pub games such as darts and dominoes are played here and there is also a quiz every Sunday evening which is open to all. *The Sun Inn, 35 The Green, Acomb, North Yorkshire, YO2 5LL. Tel: 01904 798500*

About 5 miles to the northwest of Acomb is **Beningbrough Hall** (National Trust), a baroque masterpiece from the early 18th century with 7 acres of gardens, wilderness play area, pike ponds and scenic walks. There's also a fully operational Victorian laundry which

Beningbrough Hall and Gardens

graphically demonstrates the drudgery of a 19th century washing day. A major attraction here is the permanent exhibition of more than one hundred portraits on loan from the National Portrait Gallery. Other exhibitions are often held at the Hall, - for these there is usually an additional charge.

Crockey Hill

Map 4 ref F8

4m S of York, just off the A19

Crockey Hill Farm, a 64-acre mixed farm, has been owned and personally run by Debbie and Andy Todd for the past two years. From their charming farmhouse, the couple offer excellent bed and breakfast accommodation in three en suite bedrooms. Converted from an old granary building, the rooms are comfortable and pleasantly furnished and they open onto a courtyard which certainly does not resemble a farm yard. Though no evening meals are provided,

Crockley Hill Farm

there is a hearty Yorkshire breakfast to look forward to in the morning. Ideal as an overnight stop, Crockey Hill Farm also makes the perfect base for a touring holiday of north Yorkshire and children are always welcome. *Crockey Hill Farm, Crockey Hill, York, YO1 4SN. Tel: 01904 647508*

The manifold attractions of York are just a few miles from Crockey Hill, and over to the east, on the B1228 near Elvington, is the **Yorkshire Air Museum**. A memorial to the Allied Air Forces who flew from the area in World War II, the museum celebrates the history of aviation in Yorkshire and Humberside. Housed in the original wartime buildings, the museum has recreated the authentic atmosphere of the 1940s. Aircraft on display include a rebuilt Halifax and Mosquito, and one of the last surviving Lightnings.

Acaster Malbis   Map 4 ref E8
4m S of York, off the A64 via Copmanthorpe

The village's unusual name comes from the Roman caster, or fort, of Aca that once stood here, and the Malebisse family who built the pleasing little 14th century church set in riverside meadows. At Acaster Malbis, the River Ouse on its way south to join the Humber takes a long sweeping bend. Here, with views both up and down stream, stands **The Ship Inn**, a 17th century hostelry which has probably always played a part in the history of this area. To say that the inn is character-filled is an understatement - there is an air of history dating back to a time when the river traffic was more sinister than the present pleasure boats. The Ship Inn also holds the fishing rights for the stretch of the Ouse which runs alongside the pub's car park and tickets for its use are available from the pub.

Inside, much of the decor is traditional, with stone-flagged floors in some areas, roaring fires, and plenty of maritime memorabilia. The superb conservatory can seat up to 80 at any one time and is suitable for private parties and functions. The food is of a very high

The Ship Inn

standard with a good selection on both the bar menu and a la carte menu which changes regularly. Behind the bar, traditional Yorkshire hand-pulled beers - Tetley's and Taylor's - are on tap. Also available here is overnight accommodation, with eight en suite letting rooms. One has a four-poster bed and all are tastefully furnished and very comfortable.

Run by the same people who own The Ship Inn, Paul and Elaine Eckart, is the Castle Line boat company in the centre of the city of York. The company has two river launches which offer lunchtime, supper and dinner cruises from York. *The Ship Inn, Acaster Malbis, York, YO2 1XB. Tel: 01904 703888 / 705609*

Tadcaster   Map 4 ref D8
9m SW of York, off the A64

The lovely magnesian limestone used in so many fine Yorkshire churches came from the quarries established here in Roman times. Their name for Tadcaster was simply *"Calcaria"* - limestone. By 1341, however brewing had become the town's major industry, using water from river Wharfe. Three major breweries are still based in Tadcaster: John Smiths whose bitter is the best selling ale in Britain, Samuel Smiths (established in 1758 and the oldest in Yorkshire), and the Tower Brewery, owned by Bass Charringtons. The distinctive brewery buildings dominate the town's skyline and provide the basis of its prosperity. Guided tours of the breweries are available by prior booking.

Also worth visiting is *The Ark*, the oldest building in Tadcaster dating back to the 1490s. During its long history, The Ark has served as a meeting place, a post office, an inn, a butcher's shop, and a museum. It now houses the Town Council offices and is open to the public in office hours. This appealing half-timbered building takes its name from the two carved heads on the first floor beams. They are thought to represent Noah and his wife, hence the name. Tadcaster also offers some attractive riverside walks, one of which takes you across the *Virgin Viaduct* over the River Wharfe. Built in 1849 by the great railway entrepreneur George Hudson, the viaduct was intended to be part of a direct line from Leeds to York. Before the tracks were laid however Hudson was convicted of fraud on a stupendous scale and this route was never completed.

About 4 miles southwest of Tadcaster is *Hazelwood Castle*, now owned by the Carmelite Friars who use it as a retreat and conference centre. But for more than eight centuries it was the home of the Vavasour family who built it with the lovely white limestone from their quarry at Thevesdale, - the same quarry that provided the stone for York Minster and King's College Chapel, Cambridge. The well-maintained gardens and nature trail are open every afternoon, (tea room and shop open on Sundays only), and guided tours of the Castle with its superb Great Hall and 13th century Chapel, can be arranged by telephoning 01937 832738.

Riccall
Map 4 ref F9

10m S of York, on the A19

Travelling south from York on the A19, you come to the ancient village of Riccall, mentioned in the Domesday Book and with a church that was built not long after. The south doorway of the church dates back to about 1160 and its fine details have been well-preserved by a porch added in the 15th century. The village's great moment in history came in 1066 when the gigantic King Harold Hardrada of Norway and Earl Tostig sailed this far up the Ouse with some three hundred ships. They had come to claim Northumbria from Tostig's half-brother King Harold of England but they were comprehensively defeated at the Battle of Stamford Bridge.

Riccall is popular with walkers: from the village you can either go southwards alongside the River Ouse to Selby, or strike northwards towards Bishopthorpe on the outskirts of York following the track of the dismantled York to Selby railway. This latter path is part of the 150 mile long Trans Pennine Trail linking Liverpool and Hull.

The ***Dairyman's Cottage*** is not, as might be supposed, situated in a dairy but in a quiet residential area and it is the charming home of John and Audrey Wilson. The name seemed appropriate after John's many years working as a milkman. A delightful family house, here the friendly couple offer excellent bed and breakfast accommodation in a choice of four bedrooms. Varying in size, two of the rooms have their own en suite bathrooms and all are beautifully decorated and furnished, as is the residents' lounge. Pretty as a pic-

Dairyman's Cottage

ture inside, the cottage garden is also a riot of colour throughout the summer months. There is a hearty cooked breakfast provided and the Dairyman's Cottage is within easy reach of many good eating places for the evening. Children are always welcome, and cots and high chairs are available if required. *Dairyman's Cottage, 14 Kelfield Road, Riccall, York, YO4 6PG. Tel: 01757 248532*

Skipwith   *Map 4 ref F9*
10m S of York, off the A19

St Helen's Church in Skipwith is one of the oldest churches in the area with an Anglo-Saxon tower that could well have been built between 635 and 735. **The Hare and Hounds** isn't quite so old. It dates back to the early 18th century and was, originally, a tenanted farmhouse. Though it is not certain when it became a licensed premises, its position overlooking the village green and duck pond make it an ideal place to stop for a drink and a bite to eat. Though landlord and landlady Allan and Mavis have only been here a short while, they have turned the Hare and Hounds into an increasingly popular pub with locals and visitors alike. Open all day every day,

The Hare and Hounds

as well as serving a whole range of drinks food is available from noon to 8.30pm daily. Well presented and reasonably priced, the set Sunday lunch - with a choice of three roasts - is very popular indeed. During the summer, the secluded rear beer garden is well used, as are the children's amusements, and occasional race nights and karaoke nights make a pleasant change. *Hare and Hounds, Main Street, Skipwith, North Yorkshire, YO8 7SF. Tel: 01757 288455*

Just to the south of Skipwith, the Yorkshire Wildlife Trust maintains the **Skipwith Common Nature Reserve**. This 500 acres of lowland heath is one of the last such areas remaining in the north of England and is regarded as of national importance. The principal interest is the variety of insect and birdlife, but the reserve also contains a number of ancient burial sites. For further information call 01904 659570.

Pocklington

Map 5 ref H8

10m E of York, off the A1079

Set amidst rich agricultural land with the Wolds rising to the east, Pocklington is a lively market town with an unusual layout of twisting alleys running off the market place. Its splendid church, mostly 15th century but with fragments of an earlier Norman building, certainly justifies its title as the Cathedral of the Wolds (although strictly speaking Pocklington is just outside the Wolds). William Wilberforce went to the old grammar school here and, a more dubious claim to fame, the last burning of a witch in England took place in Pocklington.

Founded in Anglo Saxon times by *"Pocela's people"*, by the time the Domesday Book was compiled Pocklington was recorded as one of the only two boroughs in the East Riding. A market followed in the 13th century, but it was the building in 1815 of a canal linking the town to the River Ouse, and the later arrival of the railway, that set the seal on the town's prosperity.

The Wellington Oak, located at Canal Head, is owned and personally run by partners Derek and Danny. Renowned throughout the area for its cuisine, this impressive establishment dates back to 1820. Today it is still charming locals and visitors and enticing them to try the excellent food and well-kept ales. The interior is very attractive with a roaring log fire and exposed brickwork adding to the character. The menus are excellent with a varied selection from which to choose. Food is served every lunch time and evening, and bookings are advisable on Saturdays and Sundays to avoid disappointment. To accompany the delicious meals, Tetleys is served along with a regular guest ale.

To the rear of the establishment, there is an acre of gardens with a stream running alongside. This is an ideal place to sit on sunny days. There is also a small site which can take five touring caravans. The Wellington Oak is a credit to its owners and is certainly a

The Wellington Oak

place to which visitors return. *The Wellington Oak, Canal Head, Pocklington, York, YO4 2NW. Tel: 01759 303854*

A popular and unusual attraction in Pocklington is the **Penny Arcadia** housed in the Ritz Cinema in the market place. *"Not so much a museum as a fun palace"* it contains a wonderful collection of penny-in-the-slot amusement machines ranging from *"What the Butler Saw"* to fortune telling and pinball machines.

A few yards from the market place is **The Martins** restaurant. Arthur Rawlings, the owner, opened the restaurant just four years ago, coming here from running a restaurant in nearby Market Weighton and prior to that running a hotel in York. With this background of over 20 years in the trade it is not surprising that The Martins has been so successful.

The Martins Restaurant

A small entrance leads visitors to the magnificent two-level dining area and a stair lift is available for the elderly or infirm. Seating up to 50 at one time, the restaurant is very attractive having been well decorated and furnished. The menus offer a good choice, from snacks to full three course meals, with the most extensive selection being available in the evening. Vegetarians are well-catered for and senior citizens can take advantage of special meal deals. Children under 12 can enjoy meals at half price and pre-school children eat free.

The Martins has become particularly known for its carvery which is offered at all times. The Martins is open 10am to 2pm, Tuesday and Wednesday; 10am to 9pm, Thursday; 10am to 10pm, Friday and Saturday; and 12 noon to 7.30pm, Sunday. Closed all day Monday. *The Martins, 5 St Peter's Square, Market Place, Pocklington, East Yorkshire, YO4 2AJ. Tel: 01759 306806*

The people of Pocklington have good reason to be grateful to Major P.M. Stewart who, on his death in 1962, bequeathed **Burnby Hall and Gardens** to the town. The eight acres of gardens are world-famous for the rare collection of water-lilies planted in the two large lakes. There are some fifty varieties and in the main flowering season from July to early September they present a dazzling spectacle. The Major and his wife had travelled extensively before settling down at Burnby and there's a small museum in the Hall displaying his collection of sporting trophies. Residents of Pocklington have free entrance to the gardens, others pay a nominal charge.

Fangfoss   Map 5 ref G7
7m E of York, off the A166 or A1079

An unusual attraction in Fangfoss village is Anthony and Pat Dew's **The Rocking Horse Shop**, part of which is a small museum with a unique collection of these favoured nursery playthings whose history goes back some three hundred years. The Dews will make a rocking horse to commission, offering a wide choice of traditional and modern designs, or they will restore tired and much-ridden horses to their former splendour.

The Carpenter's Arms is a wonderful family pub run by Carole and Adrian Hutchinson who have plenty of experience in the licensed trade. Built during the 1750s, this was a well known blacksmith's

The Carpenters Arms

before also becoming an alehouse in the early 19th century. Granted a licence in the 1870s, this is still very much the village pub and it continues to provide a venue for the locals to get together as well as offering a warm welcome to visitors. Open all day on Monday, unlike most licensed premises in the area, as well as throughout the week, The Carpenter's Arms always has two real ales available, John Smith's Bitter and Black Sheep.

The pub is also popular for the delicious menu and daily specials that are served both at lunchtimes and in the evening. Well regarded for the fine quality of the dishes, the pub specialities include home made meat pies and fresh home cooked curries. Both the lunchtime and evening menus have special selections for children, and on Monday lunchtimes the kids' meals are a set price of £1. Cosy and full of character inside, there are a number of clocks on display showing the time in London, New York and Victoria, Australia - just to keep everyone in touch with the rest of the world - and amongst the collection of antique guns hangs a sign saying *"Prices subject to change according to customer's attitude"*. Lively and friendly always, on Sunday evenings there is a quiz night, open to all, and those taking part are rewarded with a free supper whilst Monday evening is the best time to come here for a game of dominoes. *The Carpenter's Arms, Fangfoss, East Yorkshire, YO4 5QG. Tel: 01759 368222*

Bishop Wilton   Map 5 ref H7
10 miles E of York of the A166

The unspoilt village of Bishop Wilton, about five miles northeast of Fangfoss, lies at the foot of Garrowby Hill on the very edge of the Wolds. Running through its broad main street is the Bishop Wilton Beck, flanked by green banks. The Saxon Bishops of York built a palace here and used it as a country retreat. The palace has disappeared but the parish **Church of St Edith** is worth visiting for its Romanesque chancel arch and doorway, and its unusual mosaic floor made of black and white marble and modelled on one in the Vatican. The tiny pieces of marble, each no bigger than a fingernail, are cunningly arranged to create pictures of birds and scenery.

A few miles northwest of Fangfoss is the site of the **Battle of Stamford Bridge.** Everyone knows that 1066 was the year of the Battle of Hastings but, just a few days before that battle, King Harold had clashed at Stamford Bridge with his half-brother Tostig and Hardrada, King of Norway who between them had mustered some 60,000 men. On a rise near the corn mill is a stone commemorating the event with an inscription in English and Danish. Up until 1878, a Sunday in September was designated *"Spear Day Feast"*, commemorating the battle. On this day, boat-shaped pies were made bearing the impression of the fatal spear, in memory of the Saxon soldier in his boat who slew the single Norseman defending the wooden bridge. Harold's troops were triumphant but immediately after this victory they marched southwards to Hastings and a much more famous defeat.

CHAPTER SIX
Selby and North Humberside

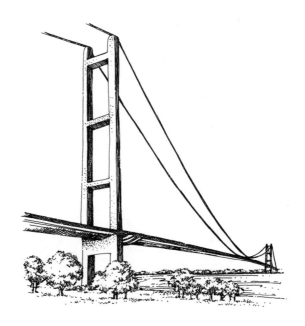

The Humber Bridge

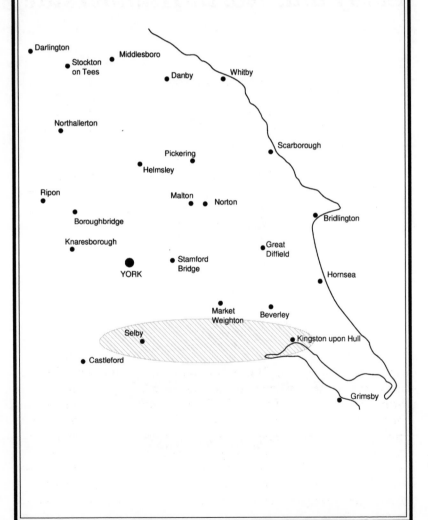

Chapter 6 - Area Covered

*For precise location of places please refer to the colour
maps found at the rear of the book.*

Darlington

Stockton
on Tees

Middlesboro

Danby

Whitby

Northallerton

Pickering

Scarborough

Helmsley

Ripon

Malton

Norton

Boroughbridge

Bridlington

Knaresborough

Great
Diffield

YORK

Stamford
Bridge

Hornsea

Market
Weighton

Beverley

Selby

Kingston upon Hull

Castleford

Grimsby

6
Selby and North Humberside

Introduction

Selby is the most southerly of the eight districts that make up the vast, sprawling county of North Yorkshire. Here, the level plains of the Vale of York stretch for miles, - rich, agricultural land watered by the four great Yorkshire rivers, Ouse, Wharfe, Derwent and Aire, and by the Selby canal. It is ideal country for walking and cycling, or for exploring the waterways on which a wide variety of rivercraft is available for hire. Just a few miles away, on the other side of the River Aire, traffic on the M62 hurtles between Leeds and Hull, but here you can still find quiet villages, inviting hostelries, and one of the country's most flamboyant stately homes, Carlton Towers.

Selby

In 1069 a young monk named Benedict, from Auxerre in France, had a vision. It's not known exactly what the vision was, but it inspired him to set sail for York. As his ship was sailing up the Ouse near Selby, three swans flew in formation across its bows. (Three swans, incidentally, still form part of the town's coat of arms). Interpreting this as a sign of the Holy Trinity, Benedict promptly went ashore and set up a preaching cross under a great oak, called the *"Stirhac"*. The small religious community he established went from strength to strength, acquiring many grants of land and, in 1100, permission to build a monastery. Over the course of the next 120 years, the great **Abbey** slowly took shape, the massively heavy Norman style of the earlier building gradually modulating into the much more delicate Early English style, all built using a lovely cream-coloured stone.

Over the centuries, this sublime church has suffered more than most. During the Civil War, it was severely damaged by Cromwell's troops who destroyed many of its statues and smashed much of its stained glass. In 1690, the central tower collapsed. For years, the Abbey was neglected and by the middle of the 18th century, a wall

Selby Abbey

had been built across the chancel so that the nave could be used as a warehouse. That wall was removed during a major restoration in the 19th century, but in 1906 there was another calamity when a disastrous fire gutted the Abbey. Visiting this serene and peaceful church today, it's difficult to believe that it has endured so many misfortunes and remained so beautiful. Throughout all the Abbey's troubles, one particular feature survived intact - the famous Washington window depicting the coat of arms of John de Washington, Prior of the Abbey around 1415 and a direct ancestor of George Washington. Prominently displayed in this heraldic device is the stars and stripes motif later adapted for the national flag of the United States.

Devotees of railway history will also want to pay their respects to Selby's old railway station. Built at the incredibly early date of 1834, it is the oldest surviving station in Britain.

Set in the centre of Selby and close to the famous Abbey are the aptly named **Abbey Vaults**. In years gone by this was a tithe barn, part of the Abbey estate, but over the years it was gradually demolished. Remaining stones have been incorporated into the walls of the pub as it is today. A smashing northern welcome awaits visitors as they enter and the pub is much larger than it initially appears. On one side is a tastefully decorated and panelled dining area, while the bar area is more cosy with lots of decorative memorabilia. Food is served each lunchtime and every evening except Sunday, while behind the bar there is a full range of Mansfield Ales. This is a lively, with regular entertainment in the form of quizzes and karaoke and, on the last Saturday of each month, live music. *The Abbey Vaults, James Street, Selby, North Yorkshire, YO8 0PY. Tel: 01757 702857*

Dove Cottages, just to the south of Selby, have to be some of the best self-catering accommodation in Yorkshire, if not in England. Found well off the main road heading south out of the town and in a secluded location, until a few years ago these two delightful cottages were completely derelict. Now, after some expert and imaginative renovation, they offer the visitor luxury accommodation set amid the rolling countryside of this wonderfully rich farming area.

Dove Cottages

Both the two cottages are furnished and decorated to the highest standards and the latest equipment has been installed so that those staying here can enjoy their holiday in this peaceful location whilst having all the modern conveniences to hand. Ideal for families with young children, care has been taken to ensure that the properties are child proof. For those interested in taking advantage of the wonderful atmosphere of Dove Cottages, Jenny Webster, the owner, is happy to supply all the literature required. *Dove Cottages, Primrose Hill Farm, Camblesforth Road, Selby, North Yorkshire, YO8 8ND. Tel: 01757 708931 / 704386*

Around Selby

Brayton
2m SW of Selby, on the A19

Map 4 ref E10

Built at the turn of the century and standing on the banks of the drive leading to Yorkshire Water's fine Victorian Pumping Station, is **Beric West Cottage**, the place to come for better bed and breakfast. This is very much a rural situation and from all corners of the cottage and its garden there are lovely views over the rolling Yorkshire countryside. Beric is still very much a family home and the hosts, Betty and Eric, ensure that all their guests, whilst experiencing luxury accommodation, also feel at home. The two guest bed-

Beric West Cottage

rooms both have en suite facilities and lots of little extras, and there is also a guest lounge. The garden around the cottage is marvellous, a true riot of colour through the spring and summer and, as well as the lily pond, there is also a lawn tennis court - now how many establishments can boast this facility? Finally, Betty's traditional cooked breakfasts are legendary and her home made preserves a definite must. Awarded 2 Crowns Highly Commended by the ETB, this is a superb place to stay whilst in the area. *Beric West Cottage, Mill Lane, Brayton, Selby, North Yorkshire, YO8 9LB. Tel: 01757 213318*

Anyone interested in remarkable churches should make the short trip from Selby to *St Mary's Church at Hemingbrough*. Built in a pale rose-coloured brick, it has an extraordinarily lofty and elegant spire soaring 190ft high and, inside, what is believed to be Britain's oldest misericord. Misericords are hinged wooden seats for the choir which were raised when they stood to sing. Medieval woodworkers delighted in adorning the underside of the seat with intricate carvings. The misericord at Hemingbrough dates back to AD1200.

Peckfield   *Map 4 ref D10*
9m W of Selby, alongside the A1

Milford Lodge Hotel lies close to the A1 and so it is an ideal place to break a journey or to use as a touring base. Purpose-built on the site of the Oakfield public house, this magnificent hotel is owned and personally managed by Shaun Sleath. There are over 40 outstanding bedrooms, all with full en suite facilities and all the modern conveniences expected by today's traveller. Nearly half the rooms are reserved as non-smoking bedrooms, and there are also rooms particularly suited to the needs of the disabled guest.

The hotel boasts one of the best chefs in the county, Chris Baxter, and the food here is certainly worth trying. From breakfast, right through to the extensive, modern dinner menu, there is a wide range of choice with something for everyone. The restaurant is open to

Milford Lodge Hotel

non-residents and so those who are unable to stay for long can still enjoy the wonderful gourmet food here. For the business guest, Milford Lodge Hotel also has extensive conference facilities and can accommodate most business requirements. All in all, the Milford Lodge Hotel is a great find that is well worth looking up. *Milford Lodge Hotel, A1 Great North Road, Peckfield, North Yorkshire, LS25 5LQ. Tel: 01977 681800 / Fax: 01977 681245*

Across the woods and meadows from the village is the 14th century **Steeton Hall Gatehouse**. Once owned by the Fairfax family, this imposing gatehouse originally formed part of a medieval castle. A forbear of the famous Cromwellian general is said to have ridden out from here on his way to carry off one of the nuns at Nun Appleton Priory to make her his bride. He was Sir William Fairfax, she was Isabel Thwaites, a wealthy heiress.

Also close by is the attractive village of **Sherburn-in-Elmet**, once the capital of the Celtic Kingdom of Elmete. Well worth visiting is All Saints' Church which stands on a hill to the west and dates from about 1120. Its great glory is the nave with its mighty Norman pillars and arcades. A curiosity here is a 15th century Janus cross which was discovered in the churchyard during the 1770s. The vicar and churchwarden of the time both claimed it as their own. Unable to resolve their dispute, they had the cross sawn in half: the two beautifully carved segments are displayed on opposite sides of the south aisle.

Temple Hirst   *Map 4 ref E10*
6m S of Selby, off the A19

Temple Hirst is a tiny village set around a loop in the River Aire. **The Sloop Inn** occupies a splendid position here amid rolling countryside and with the river flowing through the bottom of the grounds.

The Sloop Inn

Denise and Barry Kirby bought the pub in May 1997 and, in such a short time, they have made this a popular place frequented by locals and visitors alike. There is a large and beautiful beer garden with several amusements for children, and beyond there is a field set aside for campers and caravanners. Inside, the Sloop Inn is well decorated and furnished, with a cosy dining area, comfortable lounge bar, and a games room.

Though closed at lunchtime on Monday, Tuesday and Wednesday, at all other times a delicious menu of home cooked food is available which includes everything from light and tasty bar snacks to full dinners, with a special children's menu. As well as the excellent and reasonably priced menus, the Sloop Inn also serves a good range of real ales, including Tetley's and John Smith's. Well worth a visit, this delightful pub is the perfect place for a quiet drink and is very suitable for all the family. *The Sloop Inn, Main Street, Temple Hirst, North Yorkshire, YO8 8QN. Tel: 01757 270267*

About three miles to the west of Temple Hirst, near the village of West Haddlesey, is **Yorkshire Garden World**. Gardeners will find endless inspiration in these six acres of beautiful display and nursery gardens. Organically grown herbs, heathers, ornamental perennials, wild flowers and climbers are on sale; the gift shop has a huge variety of home made crafts, herbal products, Leeds pottery and garden products; and the many different gardens include a Heather and Conifer Garden, an Aromatherapy Garden, an Open Air Herb Museum, a Lover's Garden and the Hall Owl Maze for children.

Camblesforth

Map 4 ref F10

5m SE of Selby, on the A1041

In the summer of 1996 it looked as if **The Black Dog Inn** would be serving its last pint and closing down. Fortunately, Connie and Ron Wharmby thought otherwise and since taking over the pub they have turned around its fortunes in a rather dramatic fashion. Tastefully decorated and furnished, the Black Dog is a pleasant and lively place to visit and, with the addition of a conservatory, the dining area has been extended.

Open at lunchtimes and in the evening throughout the week and all day at weekends, this is a super place to come to for a glass or two of fine ale, particularly mild beer, and an excellent meal. Both the lunchtime and evening menus feature a host of delicious dishes, and curries are something of a house speciality. Every six weeks or so there is a food theme night, events which are both popular and

The Black Dog Inn

enjoyable and well worth attending. At the back of the pub is a pleasant beer garden, with a bouncy castle in summer for the children, and there is also space for five touring caravans, complete with their own facilities, and, of course, campers have the opportunity to eat and drink here. The *Black Dog Inn, Selby Road, Camblesforth, North Yorkshire, YO8 8HX. Tel: 01757 618247*

Just to the northeast of Camblesforth is **Drax** which, as well as providing Ian Fleming with a sinister sounding name for one of the villains in his James Bond novels, also provides the National Grid with more than 10% of all the electricity used in England and Wales. The largest coal-fired power station in Europe, Drax's vast cooling towers dominate the low-lying ground between the rivers Ouse and Aire. Drax power station has found an unusual way of harnessing its waste heat by channelling some of it to a huge complex of glasshouses covering twenty acres; more goes to specially heated ponds in which young eels are grown for the export market. Guided tours are available by prior arrangement.

Not to be missed while you are in this corner of the county is **Carlton Towers**, a mile or so south of Camblesforth, off the A1041. This extraordinary building, *"something between the Houses of Parliament and St Pancras Station"*, was created during the 1870s by two young English eccentrics, Henry 9th Lord Beaumont, and Edward Welby Pugin, son of the eminent Victorian architect, A.G. Pugin. They transformed a traditional Jacobean house into an exuberant mock medieval fantasy in stone, abounding with turrets, towers, gargoyles and heraldic shields. The richly-decorated, *"High Victorian"* interior, designed in the manner of medieval banqueting halls contains a minstrels' gallery and a vast Venetian drawing room. Both Beaumont and Pugin died in their forties, both bankrupt. Carlton Towers is now the Yorkshire home of the Duke of Norfolk and open to the public during the summer months.

Breighton

Map 5 ref G9

11m E of Selby, off the A163

Ye Olde Poachers Inne is a family run restaurant with a big difference. Owned and personally run by Paula and Graham Clarke with the help of their children Trevor and Sam (who are also the chefs), this old farmhouse is now a magnificent medieval restaurant and function room. The interior decor of the building sets the scene and creates a wonderful atmosphere: swords, helmets and old flintlock guns decorate the brick walls, and roaring log fires ward off the chill of cold winter nights. However, there is nothing ancient about the extensive and imaginative a la carte menu served here

Ye Olde Poachers Inne

each evening. With a fine reputation that extends far and wide, Ye Olde Poachers Inne is a wonderful place for a superb dinner. There are several house specialities and these include a fine list of fish dishes, a wonderful rack of lamb and a delicious home made Poacher's Pie. Vegetarians are well-catered for and these dishes are very much a feature of the menu rather than an afterthought. Popular in the evenings, it is advisable to book a table: the Sunday lunchtime carvery is also a wonderful feast. Ye Olde Poachers Inne is a must for anyone in the area and certainly worth going out of your way to find. *Ye Olde Poachers Inne, Main Street, Breighton, North Yorkshire, YO8 7DH. Tel: 01757 288849*

Howden Minster

A couple of miles south of Breighton are the striking remains of **Wressle Castle**, built in 1380 for Sir Henry Percy and the only example of a fortified house surviving in East Yorkshire. At the end of the Civil War, three of the castle's sides were pulled down and much of the rest was destroyed by a fire in 1796. But two massive towers with walls 6ft thick, the hall and kitchens remain. The Castle is not open to the public but there are excellent views from the village road and from a footpath that runs alongside the River Derwent. A fine old windmill nearby is an extra visual bonus.

Howden   Map 5 ref G10
11m E of Selby, on the A63

Despite the fact that its chancel collapsed in 1696 and has not been used for worship ever since, **Howden Minster** is still one of the largest parish churches in East Yorkshire and also one of its most impressive, cathedral-like in size. The ruins of its former chapter house have been described as one of the most exquisite little buildings in England, lavishly decorated with a wealth of carved mouldings.

When the medieval Prince-Bishops of Durham held sway over most of northern England, they built a palace at Howden which they used as a stopping-place during their semi-royal progresses and as a summer residence. The Hall of that 14th century palace still stands, although much altered now.

The town itself is a pleasing jumble of narrow flagged and setted streets, with a picturesque brick and stone market hall in the market place. The celebrated aircraft designer Barnes Wallis knew Howden well: he lived here while working on the R100 airship which was built at Hedon airfield nearby. It made its maiden flight in 1929 and successfully crossed the Atlantic.

The Cross Keys, on the edge of the centre of Howden, is a late 19th century pub where, on the brickwork covering an old exterior door, visitors can see the initials etched by punters impatient for the pub to open. Today's drinkers will not be so frustrated as the pub is open from 3pm until closing time, Monday to Friday, and from noon at weekends. Landlady Jayne and husband Steve have been here for only a short time but they have turned round the fortunes of The Cross Keys and transformed it into a popular inn with a friendly atmosphere.

In the summer months, the beer garden proves a popular attraction, not only for the seclusion it offers but also for the small aviary and the barbecue to which people can bring their own food. Inside,

The Cross Keys

the bar area and games room are both cosy with roaring fires to brighten up even the chilliest of evenings. Although no food is served at The Cross Keys, a fine range of beers, ales and lagers, as well as the usual wines and spirits, can be found, including traditional Tetley's ale. An excellent place at any time of year and, for those who enjoy a sing song, Karaoke is a popular attraction once a month on Saturday evening and Sunday lunchtime. *The Cross Keys, 2 Hull Road, Howden, East Yorkshire, DN14 7AQ. Tel: 01430 431391*

Howden Art and Craft Centre

Howden Art and Craft Centre was opened in November 1992 by Margaret Herbert in renovated garages which stood on the site of an old Congregational church. Since then, things have snowballed and the Centre is now one of the leading craft shops in the north of

England. Stocking everything that the keen artist and needleworker could possible need, new products arrive at the Centre every day and other crafts now catered for include candle-making, decoupage, quilting, flower arranging and chair seating. Here too is the Pegasus Studio, a meeting place for local societies but also a place where exhibitions are held and, during the winter, a wide variety of workshops and classes are held by visiting tutors. If that was not enough, Margaret has also opened the charming Pastimes Tearoom - she was given a Civic Award for the outstanding renovation of the building in which it is housed. Here visitors can enjoy a cup of tea or coffee whilst tucking into a mouthwatering array of home made scones, cakes and light meals. The facilities for disabled visitors are excellent at the Howden Art and Craft Centre and coach parties are welcomed. *Howden Art and Craft Centre, 35-37 Bridgegate, Howden, East Yorkshire, DN14 7JG. Tel / Fax: 01430 430807*

Standing on the main A614 between Howden and Holme-on-Spalding-Moor is the former coaching inn, the ***Royal Oak***. Although the pub has stood on this site for over 250 years, the present owners, Barry and Elaine, only arrived in November 1996. They have already made their mark though, giving the Royal Oak a new lease of life through their hard work and creative talent. Today, it offers the traveller an ideal place to stop and enjoy excellent food in mod-

The Royal Oak

ern and stylish surroundings. The establishment encompasses an inn, restaurant and a cafe, so whether you fancy a quiet drink and bar snack in the bar, a first class meal in the restaurant, or a cup of tea and a quick bite in the cafe, the Royal Oak is ideal. Open daily through the summer, closed Mondays in the winter. *The Royal Oak, Holme Road, Howden, East Yorkshire, DN14 7NA. Tel: 01430 430563*

Hull and North Humberside

Mercilessly battered by the Luftwaffe during World War II when 7,000 of its people were killed and 92% of its houses suffered bomb damage, Hull has risen phoenix-like from those ashes and is now the fastest-growing port in England. The port area extends for seven miles along the Humber, with ten miles of quays servicing a constant flow of commercial traffic arriving from, or departing for, every quarter of the globe. Every day, a succession of vehicle ferries link the city to the European gateways of Zeebrugge and Rotterdam. Hull is unmistakably part of Yorkshire but it also has the free-wheeling, open-minded character of a cosmopolitan port.

Hull's history as an important port goes back to 1293 when Edward I, travelling north on his way to hammer the Scots, stopped off here and immediately recognized the potential of the muddy junction where the River Hull flows into the Humber. The king bought the land from the monks of Meaux Abbey at the usual royal discount and the settlement thenceforth was known as *"Kinges town upon Hull"*. The port grew steadily through the centuries and at one time had the biggest fishing fleet of any port in the country with more than 300 trawlers on its register. The port's rather primitive facilities were greatly improved by the construction of a state-of-the-art dock in 1778. Now superseded, that dock has been converted into the handsome Queens Gardens, one of the many attractive open spaces created by this flower-conscious city which also loves lining its streets with trees, setting up fountains here and there and planting flower beds in any unoccupied space. Waymarked walks such as the *Maritime Heritage Trail* and the *Fish Pavement Trail* make the most of the city's dramatic waterfront.

A visit to Hull is an exhilarating experience at any time of the year but especially so in October. Back in the late 1200s the city was granted a charter to hold an autumn fair. This began as a fairly modest cattle and sheep mart but over the centuries it burgeoned into the largest gathering of its kind in Europe. Hull Fair is now a nine day extravaganza occupying a 14 acre site crammed with every imaginable variety of entertainment.

That takes care of October, but Hull also hosts an Easter Festival, an International Festival (some 300 events from mid-June to late July), a Jazz on the Waterfront celebration (August), an International Sea Shanty Festival (September) and a Literature Festival in November. Throughout the rest of the year Hull's tourism office modestly suggests you explore its *"Magnificent Seven"*, - a quite remarkable collection of historic houses, art galleries and museums.

Perhaps the most evocative is the **Wilberforce House Museum** in the old High Street. William Wilberforce was born here, from here he and his father lavished thousands of pounds in bribes to get William elected as Hull's Member of Parliament. Nothing unusual about that kind of corruption at the time, but William then redeemed himself by his resolute opposition to slavery. His campaign took more than thirty years and William was already on his deathbed before a reluctant Parliament finally outlawed the despicable trade. The museum presents a shaming history of the slave trade and a more uplifting story of William Wilberforce's efforts to eliminate it for ever.

The Ferens Art Gallery houses a sumptuous collection of paintings that range from European Old Masters (including some Canalettos and Franz Hals) to challenging contemporary art; the **Town Docks Museum** celebrates seven centuries of Hull's maritime heritage and includes a fine collection of scrimshaw; at **Streetlife Transport Museum** you will be taken back to the days of horse-drawn carriages, steam trains, trams and penny-farthing cycles. There are curiosities such as the *"Velocipede"*, the Automobile a Vapeur, - an early steam driven car - and Lady Chesterfield's ornamental sleigh, caparisoned with a swan, rearing unicorn and a panoply of bells to herald her approach.

You will encounter a marvel of a different kind if you come by road to Hull from the south and drive over one of the most impressive bridges on earth. Opened in 1981, the **Humber Bridge** is the world's longest single-span bridge with an overall length of 2,428yds, (2,220m). That means that for more than a third of a mile only four concrete pillars, two at each end, are saving you from a watery death. From these huge pylons, 510ft (155m) high, gossamer cables of thin-wired steel support a gently curving roadway. Both sets of pylons rise vertically, but because of the curvature of the earth they actually lean away from each other by several inches. The bridge is particularly striking at night when the vast structure is floodlit.

Before leaving the city, one should mention two of its more unusual features. Firstly, visitors to Hull some become aware of its unique public telephones. They are still those traditional, curvy-topped, heavily-barred boxes but with the distinctive difference that Hull's are all painted a gleaming white. What isn't apparent is that by some bureaucratic quirk, Hull has the only municipally owned telephone company in Britain. The second unusual feature: in Nelson Street you can avail yourself of award-winning loos. These spotless conveniences, complete with hanging baskets of flowers, have become a tourist attraction in their own right.

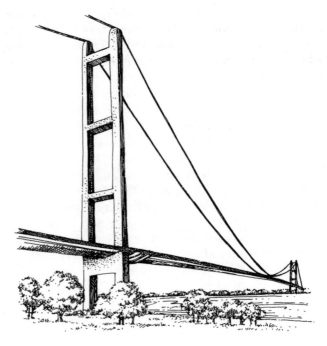

The Humber Bridge

Hessle

Map 6 ref J10

5m W of Hull, off the A63

At Hessle, the River Humber narrows and it was here that the Romans maintained a ferry, the *"Transitus Maximus"* a vital link in the route between Lincoln and York. The river is now spanned by the Humber Bridge whose massive pylons soar more than 500ft above the village. The great bridge dwarfs **Cliff Mill**, built in 1810 to mill the local chalk. It remained wind-driven until 1925 when a gas engine was installed. The windmill is no longer working but it remains one of the outstanding attractions within the **Humber Bridge Country Park**. This well laid out park gives visitors a true back to nature tour a short distance from one of modern man's greatest feats of engineering. The former chalk quarry has been attractively landscaped with a nature trail, extensive walks through woodlands and meadows, picnic and play areas, and picturesque water features.

Weir Lodge is the wonderful home of Delphine and John Robertson and, for those lucky enough to discover this hidden gem, it is also a first class guest house. The house was built in 1773 and a wing was added in Victorian times so the original name, Quaint Cottage, reflects the charm of the building, not its size. Surrounded by trees and shrubbery, this is an ideal spot for relaxing though it is also within easy driving distance of Hull and many of Yorkshire's attractions.

Perhaps the reason for the air of tranquillity of the house is down to the blessing it received, supposedly when the house was built. The verse, written on an interior wall, which Delphine is happy to show anyone interested, is said to have protected the house from witches and other ghoulish things of the night.

Weir Lodge

Bed and breakfast accommodation is provided for weary travellers in three delightfully and individually decorated bedrooms, each with its own bathroom. However, Weir Lodge is not suitable for children or the disabled, and it is also a non-smoking property. *Weir Lodge, Tower Hill, Hessle, East Yorkshire, HU13 0SG. Tel: 01482 648564*

Newport   *Map 5 ref H10*
15m W of Hull, on the B1230 (via junc. 38, M62)
Newport is built on clay and once had a flourishing trade in bricks which it transported along the Market Weighton canal. Many of the old clay pits are now filled with flood water and are popular with anglers and naturalists. In some of them there have been sightings of the rare great crested newt.

The *Jolly Sailor*, in the centre of Newport village, was rebuilt at the turn of the century and is surprisingly large and roomy inside. A real, warm Yorkshire welcome awaits all visitors, whether

The Jolly Sailor

new or familiar, from the hosts Bill and Jill Grant. Not only does the Jolly Sailor serve an excellent selection of ales and beers, the restaurant - which is open all week except for Monday lunchtime - offers an interesting and exciting menu of tasty dishes that certainly won't break the bank. A busy and friendly pub where no-one is a stranger for long, particularly on the Quiz Nights (Tuesdays, Thursdays and Sundays), the Jolly Sailor is probably unique in having a collection of Jack Daniels' bottles hanging from the ceiling. Unfortunately, (or fortunately), empty, the bottles make an interesting talking point. *The Jolly Sailor, Main Road, Newport, Brough, East Yorkshire, HU15 2RG. Tel: 01430 449191*

North Cave

Map 5 ref I9

13m W of Hull, on the B1230 (via junc. 38, M62)

In this unspoilt farming community on the edge of the Wolds, you'll find the magnificent **White Hart** public house, dating back to the late 18th century and with plenty to offer the visitor. After gaining experience locally in the licensing trade, Val and Pam teamed up and took over running the White Hart just 18 months ago. Full of character inside, the success of the pub is due to the superb blend of fine ales, excellent food, and a warm and friendly atmosphere: a real tribute to the hard work of Pam and Val.

Well worth a visit, the White Hart has a winning formula for an enjoyable evening out. Tasty, freshly prepared meals are served between 5pm and 8pm each evening (9pm on Fridays and Saturdays)

The White Hart

and there are a variety of extra features to help the evening go with a swing, including quiz nights on Sundays and Country and Western nights on Wednesdays. The White Hart also serves lunches during the week and on Saturdays from 11.30am to 2pm, and on Sundays from 12 noon to 7pm. There is, of course, plenty of hand-pulled real ale on tap. *The White Hart, Westgate, North Cave, East Yorkshire, HU15 2NJ. Tel: 01430 422432*

About five miles north of North Cave is the **Northern Shire Horse Centre** in the village of North Newbald, off the A1034. As well as admiring these mighty creatures in their natural surroundings, you can browse through an interesting collection of horse-drawn vehicles and implements, a harness room with a striking display of horse brasses and other artefacts, and a Bygones Museum. A Victorian kitchen, a Costume Museum and a tea room are among the many other attractions.

The nearby village of Brantingham, just off the A63, is worth a short diversion to see its remarkable war memorial, once described as *"lovingly awful"*. Conceived on a monumental scale, the memorial was built using masonry re-cycled from Hull's old Guildhall when that was being reconstructed in 1914. Various stone urns placed around the village came from the same source.

Welton *Map 5 ref J10*
10m W of Hull, off the A63

In this pretty village, a stream flows past the green, under bridges and into a tree-lined duck pond. The imposing Welton Grange, with its Venetian style windows, was built in 1741 for a Hull merchant. Indeed, most of Welton was a retreat for the wealthy shipping merchants of Hull, a fact reflected in the architecture.

The Church of St Helen dates from Norman times and is noted for its 13th century doorway and the Pre-Raphaelite windows made by William Morris' company of craftsmen. In the graveyard stands a memorial to Jeremiah Found, a resilient local reputed to have out-lived eight wives.

The notorious highwayman Dick Turpin was not a local but his villainous, if romantic, career came to an end at Welton village when he was apprehended inside *The Green Dragon* inn. Local legend has it that this establishment gave him hospitality before he was taken off to the magistrates at Beverley who committed him to the Assizes at York where he was found guilty and hanged in 1739. The inn has since been carefully restored and today can provide superb accommodation in traditional surroundings. There are 11 rooms, all with en suite facilities and beautifully furnished. They are well-equipped with colour television, drinks tray, trouser press, telephone and complimentary newspaper.

The Green Dragon Hotel

The bar areas are comfortable and spacious and the service excellent. Here visitors can enjoy a delicious pint from the Mansfield Brewery and choose a meal from the extensive menu. All the dishes are freshly prepared and come in hearty portions. Children and vegetarians are also catered for. An ideal place to stay, conveniently situated for the city of Hull. *The Green Dragon Hotel, Cowgate, Welton, Hull, HU15 1NB. Tel: 01482 666700 / Fax: 01482 667808*

Situated just on the outskirts of the village, only five minutes from the main road leading into Hull, is the ***Welton Heights Riding Centre.*** For hacking, riding lessons and livery, riders and beginners need look no further. Owned and personally run by Dallas Tongue, herself an experienced rider, Welton Heights is a place where

Welton Heights Riding Centre

novices and competent riders mix in a family-like atmosphere. The Centre is home to a variety of horses, to suit all sizes and abilities. Hacks last from one hour upwards and a short lesson is given to assess the standard of riders before the hack starts. There is an outdoor arena and a cross country course in addition to the many bridleways in the surrounding area. Disabled riders are very welcome, with advance notice. During the summer months, camping/riding holidays are available. For those who like riding, this is a great place to try. *Welton Heights Riding Centre, Beverley Road, Welton, Hull, HU15 1QR. Tel: 01482 665248*

Swanland   *Map 6 ref J10*
7m W of Hull, on the B1231
The delightfully named ***Swan and Cygnet*** can be found, rather appropriately, in Swanland overlooking the village pond, which is itself frequently visited by swans, ducks, and other wild birds. This popular pub also has superb views across to the Humber Bridge. A property of the Mansfield Brewery Company, customers can be sure of getting a good pint and may also want to try some of the great pub food: the menu is varied and exceedingly well priced. To the

The Swan and Cygnet

rear is a beer garden and there is a large off-road private car park. *Swan and Cygnet, Main Street, Swanland, North Ferriby, HU14 3QP. Tel: 01482 634571*

About five miles north of Swanland, just off the A164, is **Skidby Mill**, built in 1821 and one of the few surviving working tower mills in the country. A listed building, it stands on a hill above the village, seven storeys high a landmark for miles around. Its onion-shaped cap is complete with four sails, each weighing over 1.25 tonnes, and fantail. On most Sundays, the Skidby miller demonstrates his ancient skill and visitors can buy his stone-ground flour and special recipes to make the best use of it. The old mill buildings nearby house a museum of vintage implements and materials used in corn production and milling.

North Ferriby
9m W of Hull, off the A63

Map 6 ref J10

The **Duke of Cumberland**, in the centre of North Ferriby, is a large public house which, though rather imposing from the outside, offers a warm and friendly welcome. Decorated with a whole host of memorabilia including many prints, the cosy and intimate interior is the ideal place to enjoy a quiet glass or two of beer with friends and, during fine weather, there is a large beer garden to the rear. As well as being renowned locally for its fine range of beers, the Duke of Cumberland has an excellent reputation for its food. Interesting and imaginative, the regularly changing menu has something for

The Duke of Cumberland

everyone and will satisfy the largest of appetites. One of the Mansfield Brewery inns, this, like the others in the chain, offers excellent hospitality for all the family. *The Duke of Cumberland, High Street, North Ferriby, Nr. Hull, HU14 3JP Tel: 01482 631592*

CHAPTER 7
Bridlington & the Wolds

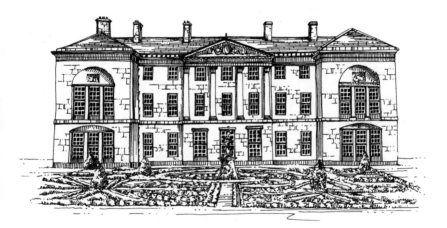

Sledmere House

Chapter 7 - Area Covered

For precise location of places please refer to the colour maps found at the rear of the book.

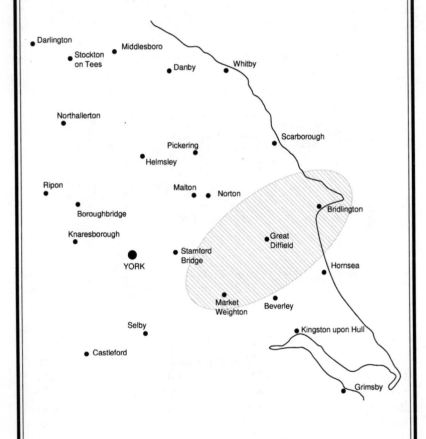

7
Bridlington & the Wolds

Introduction

"Fold upon fold of encircling hills, piled rich and golden" - such was the author Winifred Holtby's fond memory of the Wolds landscape. She was born in 1898 in Rudston on the northern edge of the Wolds, a village dominated by the prehistoric **Rudston Monolith**. This colossal block of stone, a daunting symbol of some misty pagan belief, stands challengingly close to Rudston's Christian parish church. Twenty-five feet (7.6m) high, it is the tallest standing stone in Britain. Winifred Holtby later became a leading figure in London literary circles, editor of the influential magazine Time and Tide, but in her own books it was those *"rich and golden"* hills that still enthralled her. In her most successful novel, *"South Riding"*, the fictional Riding is unmistakably recognisable as the Wolds amongst whose gently rolling acres she had spent her childhood.

The Wolds are a great crescent of chalk hills that sweep round from the coast near Flamborough Head to the outskirts of Hull. There were settlers here some 10,000 years ago, - but never very many. In the early 1700s, Daniel Defoe described the area as *"very thin of towns and people"* and also noted the *"great number of sheep"*. Little has changed: the Wolds remain an unspoilt tract of scattered farmsteads and somnolent villages with one of the lowest population densities in the country. Artists remark on the striking quality of the light and air, and on the long views that open up, perhaps across undulating hills to the twin towers of Beverley Minster or to the great towers of the Minster at York. The Wolds never rise above

800ft but the open landscape makes them particularly vulnerable to winter snowstorms: children may be marooned in their schools, the dipping and twisting country roads can be blocked for weeks at a time.

Bridlington

Bridlington lies at the northern tip of the crescent of hills that form the Wolds. The old town lies a mile inland from the bustling seaside resort that has been understandably popular since early Victorian times. The attractions of a vast, ten mile stretch of sandy beach distract most visitors from the less obvious beauties of **Bridlington Priory** in the old town. The Priory was once one of the wealthiest in England but it was ruthlessly pillaged during the Reformation. Externally it is somewhat unprepossessing, but step inside and the majestic 13th century nave is unforgettably impressive. A corner of the Priory churchyard recalls one of the most tragic days in the town's history. During a fearsome gale in January 1871, a whole fleet of ships foundered along the coast. Bridlington's lifeboat was launched but within minutes it was *"smashed to matchwood"*: most of its crew perished. Twenty bodies were washed ashore and later buried in the Priory churchyard: it was estimated that ten times as many souls found only a watery grave. This awesome tragedy is still recalled each year with a solemn service of remembrance when the lifeboat is drawn through the town.

Queen Henrietta Maria's visit to Bridlington was not as tragic, but it was certainly quite exciting. In February 1643, she landed here from a Dutch ship laden with arms and aid for her beleaguered husband, Charles I. Parliamentary naval vessels were in hot pursuit and having failed to capture their quarry, bombarded the town. Their cannonballs actually hit the Queen's lodging. Henrietta was forced to take cover in a ditch where, as she reported in a letter to her husband, *"the balls sang merrily over our heads, and a sergeant was killed not 20 paces from me"*. At this point Her Majesty deemed it prudent to retreat to the safety of Boynton Hall, three miles inland and well beyond the range of the Parliamentary cannon.

These stirring events, and many others in the long history of Bridlington and its people, are vividly brought to life with the help of evocative old paintings, photographs and artefacts in the **Bayle Museum**. Quite apart from its fascinating exhibits the museum is well worth visiting for its setting inside the old gatehouse to the town, built around 1390.

Also in the old part of Bridlington, on the High Street, you will find **Burlingtons**. Part of the building in which this restaurant is housed dates back to the 16th century and was formerly cottages. David Hall, one of the present owners, took over 7 years ago, coming from a position as head chef at a local country house hotel. Together with his wife Judy this was his first solo venture, which has been a great success. The reputation of the restaurant reaches far beyond Bridlington and many regulars travel quite some distance to enjoy a meal here.

The restaurant has been divided up into three separate areas. On entering, you will first come to the comfortable lounge area which is ideal for a drink before or after your meal. The other two areas are for dining and both are cosy and intimate. The food is of a superlative quality and David has won many awards. The menu offers an

Burlingtons

excellent selection but the chef's speciality is fish. A popular dish is the Triple Dish Platter which features a choice of seven fish dishes - from which you have to choose three! The house specials include Guinea Fowl, cooked in two different ways, - the breast in brandy and tarragon, and the leg in red wine with bacon - and 'Jamaican Duck' with caramelised pineapple in a plum sauce with a hint of ginger and a dash of rum.

The restaurant seats 40 people and is open, evenings only, from Tuesday to Saturday (inclusive) and for Sunday lunch. The interior is themed around teddy bears with hundreds of ornaments, teddies and pictures of teddy bears on display. Between 6.30 and 7.30 each evening there is an 'Early Bear' hour when two and three course meals are available at a special price. Booking is recommended at weekends. *Burlingtons, 91-93 High Street, Bridlington, East Yorkshire, YO16 4PN. Tel: 01262 400383*

At South Pier in the centre of Bridlington you will find **Rags Restaurant and Dyls Hotel**. This fine establishment is owned by Les Dyl and Julie Shackleton who have established reputations in their own fields, both outside of the catering business. Les Dyl may be remembered by many as the former international Rugby League player noted for his speed and ball handling ability. He spent 14 years in his sporting career, many spent playing for Leeds, before going on to running a bar in Spain and managing two Golf Clubs. Julie is a talented singer and participates in local amateur dramatics. In exchange for buying her a drink she'll even give you a song - it will be money well spent!

Rags Restaurant and Dyls Hotel

In the year since Les and Julie opened Rags Restaurant and Dyls Hotel they have established a new reputation for offering excellent food and luxurious accommodation. The restaurant can seat 70 and is open for lunches through the week, every evening and all day on Sunday. The menu is wide-ranging, catering to all tastes, and although the restaurant is quite large, it can get very busy at weekends, so it is advisable to book. If you want to try something a little less formal, the Bulletin Bar serves bar snacks. The bar area is decorated with pictures and cuttings from Les and Julie's careers and so makes an ideal conversation point. The superb accommodation comprises six en suite double bedrooms, three of which offer harbour views. *Rags Restaurant and Dyls Hotel, South Pier, Bridlington, East Yorkshire, YO15 3AN. Tel: 01262 400355*

Just to the north of Bridlington is **Sewerby Hall**, a monumental mansion built on the cusp of the Queen Anne and early Georgian years, between 1714 and 1720. Set in 50 acres of garden and parkland, (where there's also a small zoo), the house was first opened to the public in 1936 by Amy Johnson, the dashing, Yorkshire-born pilot who had captured the public imagination by her daring solo flights to South Africa and Australia. The Museum here houses some fascinating memorabilia of Amy's pioneering feats along with displays of motor vehicles, archaeological finds and some remarkable paintings amongst which is perhaps the most famous portrait of Queen Henrietta Maria, wife of Charles I. Queen Henrietta loved this romantic image of herself as a young, carefree woman, but during the dark days of the Civil War she felt compelled to sell it to raise funds for the doomed Royalist cause which ended with her husband's execution. After passing through several hands, this haunting portrait of a queen touched by tragedy found its last resting place at Sewerby Hall.

Around Bridlington

Flamborough *Map 8 ref M6*
5m NE of Bridlington, on the B1255.

At Flamborough Head, sea and land are locked in an unremitting battle. At the North Landing, huge, foam-spumed waves roll in between gigantic cliffs, slowly but remorselessly washing away the shoreline. Paradoxically, the outcome of this elemental conflict is to produce one of the most picturesque locations on the Yorkshire coast, much visited and much photographed.

Victorian travel writers loved Flamborough. Not just because of its dramatic scenery, but what about the people! They were so clannish and and believed in such strange superstitions! No boat would ever set sail on a Sunday, wool could not be wound in lamplight, anyone who mentioned a hare or pig while baiting the fishing lines was inviting doom. No fisherman would leave harbour unless he was wearing a navy-blue jersey, knitted by his wife in a cable, diamond mesh peculiar to the village and still worn today. Every year the villagers would slash their way through Flamborough in a sword-dancing frenzy introduced here in the 8th century by the Vikings. Eventually, local fishermen grew weary of this primitive role so although the sword dance still takes place it is now performed by boys from the primary school, accoutred in white trousers, red caps and the traditional navy-blue jerseys.

Flamborough's parish church contains two interesting monuments. One is the tomb of Sir Marmaduke Constable which shows him with his chest cut open to reveal his heart being devoured by a toad. The knight's death in 1518 had been caused, the story goes, by his swallowing the toad which had been drowsing in Sir Marmaduke's lunchtime pint of ale, apparently. The creature then devoured his heart. The other notable monument is a statue of St Oswald, patron saint of fishermen. This fishing connection is renewed every year, on the second Sunday in October, by a service dedicated to the *Harvest of the Sea*, when the area's sea-farers gather together in a church decorated with crab pots and fishing nets.

Flamborough Head's first, and England's oldest surviving *lighthouse*, is the octagonal chalk tower on the landward side of the present lighthouse. Built in 1674, its beacon was a basket of burning coal. The lighthouse that is still in use was built in 1806. Originally signalling four white flashes, developments over the years have included a fog horn in 1859 and in more recent years, a signal of radio bleeps. Until it was automated in 1995, it was the last manned lighthouse on the east coast.

Situated in this historic coastal village is an outstanding public house, *The Seabirds*, owned and personally run by Jean and Geoff for the past seven years. Dating back to the early 19th century, The

The Seabirds

Seabirds was once a coaching inn where teams of horses were changed. Originally a hotel with accommodation and stabling, it is now a public house with a reputation for serving excellent food and a fine, ever-changing selection of real ales. The menu certainly offers a good choice, catering for all tastes, and the dishes are reasonably priced. The specials board is well worth studying as this is where the chef, Ben Massey, really excels. Food is available throughout the establishment, but there is also a separate dining area for which it is advisable to book at weekends. The bar serves Boddington's and John Smith's with an additional guest ale. *The Seabirds, Tower Street, Flamborough, East Yorkshire, YO15 1PD. Tel: 01262 850242*

Just to the north of Flamborough is **Danes Dyke**, a huge rampart four miles long designed to cut off the headland from hostile invaders. The Danes had nothing to do with it, the dyke was in place long before they arrived. Sometime during the Bronze or Stone Age, early Britons constructed this extraordinary defensive ditch. A mile and a quarter of its southern length is open to the public as a Nature Trail.

Hunmanby   Map 8 ref K5
3m SW of Filey, between the A165 and A1039

Here's a question worthy of Trivial Pursuits: *"On which vehicle was the wing mirror first used?"*. Your answer is almost certainly wrong unless you know about the grave of a 1st century British charioteer uncovered at Hunmanby in 1907. Along with his bones, those of his horses, and fragments of the chariot wheels was a rectangular strip of shiny metal: archaeologists are convinced that this was fixed to the side of the chariot as a mirror so that the driver could see the competitors behind him.

Another curiosity in Hunmanby is the village lock-up with two cells and tiny windows designed for human miscreants, and next to it a circular stone pinfold intended for straying cattle.

In this typical and quaint North Yorkshire village, a good pint and excellent food can be relished at **The White Swan**. Standing opposite the parish church, it is thought that the building was originally a farm, later became a courtroom, then a coaching inn before it was a public house. The restaurant at the back of the pub used to be the courtroom for the Manor of Hunmanby, though the only orders issued these days are for the delicious food served there. In the summer months, lunches are served in the restaurant, otherwise it is open for dinner between 7pm and 9pm whilst bar meals are served throughout the day. The White Swan has five bedrooms, one a family room en suite. Alan and Dorothy have been hosts here for the

The White Swan

past six years and will make you welcome. Various entertainments such as quiz nights and live bands are a regular feature. *The White Swan, 1 Church Hill, Hunmanby, Scarborough, North Yorkshire, YO14 0JU Tel: 01723 890232*

Bempton

Map 8 ref L6

3m N of Bridlington, on the B1229

Bempton Cliffs, 400ft high, mark the northernmost tip of the great belt of chalk that runs diagonally across England from the Isle of Wight to Flamborough Head. The sheer cliffs at Bempton provide an ideal nesting place for huge colonies of fulmars, guillemots, puffins and Britain's largest seabird, the gannet, with a wingspan 6ft wide. In Victorian times, a popular holiday sport was to shoot the birds from boats. Above them, crowds gathered to watch gangs of 'climmers' make a hair-raising descent by rope down the cliffs to gather the birds' eggs. Most were sold for food, but many went to egg collectors. The 'climmers' also massacred kittiwakes in their thousands: kittiwake feathers were highly prized as accessories for hats and for stuffing mattresses. The first Bird Protection Act of 1869 was specifically designed to protect the kittiwakes at Bempton: a ban on collecting eggs here didn't come into force until 1954. Bempton Cliffs are now an RSPB bird sanctuary, a refuge during the April to August breeding season for more than 200,000 seabirds making this the largest colony in Britain.

Just a short stroll from the cliffs where in season it is possible to see guillemots and puffins nesting is **The White Horse Inn**. The pub was built in 1938 and features an unusual blue roof but it was lucky to survive the bombing during World War II. The area was often attacked due to the RAF base nearby, and to prevent the building from standing out the roof had to be painted black.

Today this is a delightfully welcoming establishment owned and run by Peter and Rose Ellen Tyas for the past six years. The bar offers an excellent range of ales and food is available at lunchtimes

The White Horse Inn

and in the evenings. The White Horse can also offer overnight accommodation in two cosy twin rooms. There are occasional special events such as race nights and karaoke evenings - ring for details - and every Tuesday there is a pub quiz open to all. *The White Horse Inn, High Street, Bempton, Bridlington, East Yorkshire, YO15 1HB. Tel: 01262 850266*

Carnaby   *Map 8 ref L6*
4m SW of Bridlington, on the A166

Leaving Bridlington on the A166 will shortly bring you to **John Bull - World of Rock** which has become a premier tourist attraction in this part of East Yorkshire and really is a great day out. Whether you are young or old, you will be fascinated as you discover the history and delights of rock making. The older generation will particularly revel in the smell of the old-fashioned way of making toffee and the interesting bygone displays. Animation and taped conversation accompany you as you explore the establishment which is described as a total sensory experience. You can even try your hand at making a personalised stick of rock.

As you enter you will discover an imaginative picture show in which the managing director's grandfather, the founder of the business, tells how the company was established and came to be called John Bull. You then walk through into where the rock is actually made and watch the process from raw ingredients to the finished product while a guide provides a commentary. From here you pass the original shop, transported here from Prince's Street, and a Victorian kitchen which shows how the rock was made many years ago. The next section covers the history of sweet making, and there are a number of puzzles specially designed for children. The next

John Bull - World of Rock

stop is Charlie's Chocolate Room where children can make their own chocolate lolly - mum and dad are not allowed in here! Next, there is a section devoted to fudge and toffee-making with videos of the stages that are involved. Finally (phew!) there is a large shop where souvenirs of your visit can be purchased. If you don't wish to go on the factory tour, the factory shop - where rejects and novelties are for sale - has no admission charge. There is now also a superb cafeteria serving hot and cold dishes and beverages. This is a unique and educational attraction that is well worth a visit. *John Bull - World of Rock, Lancaster Road, Carnaby, Bridlington, East Yorkshire, YO15 3QY. Tel: 01262 678525*

Burton Agnes

Map 8 ref K6

6m SW of Bridlington, on the A166

The overwhelming attraction in this unspoilt village is the sublime Elizabethan mansion, Burton Agnes Hall, but visitors should not ignore **Burton Agnes Manor House** (English Heritage), a rare example of a Norman house: a building of great historical importance but burdened with a grimly functional architecture, almost 800 years old, that chills one's soul. As Lloyd Grossman might say, 'How could anyone live in a house like this?'.

Burton Agnes Hall is much more appealing: an outstanding Elizabethan house, built between 1598 and 1610 and little altered, Burton Agnes is particularly famous for its splendid Jacobean gatehouse, wondrously decorated ceilings and overmantels carved in oak, plaster and alabaster. It also has a valuable collection of paintings and furniture from between the 17th and 19th centuries - including

Burton Agnes Hall

a portrait of Oliver Cromwell warts and all - and a large collection of Impressionist paintings. The gardens are extensive with over 2,000 plants, a maze and giant board games in the Coloured Gardens. Other visitor facilities include a new ice-cream parlour, a dried-flower and herb shop, a children's animal corner, and an artists' studio. A very popular addition is the plant sales where numerous uncommon varieties can be obtained. *"The Impressionist Cafe"*, open throughout the Hall's season, seats 64 inside and, in good weather,

56 outside. Non-smoking, but licensed and offering only the very best in home cooking. The scones are particularly delicious. An interesting day out for all the family. *Burton Agnes Hall, Burton Agnes, Driffield, East Yorkshire, YO25 0ND. Tel: 01262 490324 / Fax: 01262 490513*

Great Driffield   *Map 8 ref J7*
13m SW of Bridlington, on the A166

On the edge of the Wolds, Great Driffield is a busy little market town at the heart of an important corn growing area. A cattle market is held here every Thursday; a general market on both Thursday and Saturday, and the annual agricultural show has been going strong since 1854. All Saints Parish Church, dating back to the 12th century has some lovely stained glass windows portraying local nobility and one of the highest towers in the county.

Great Driffield was once the capital of the Saxon Kingdom of Deira, a vast domain extending over the whole of Northumbria and Yorkshire. It was a King of Deira who, for administrative convenience, divided the southern part of his realm into three parts, 'thriddings', a word which gradually evolved into the famous 'Ridings' of Yorkshire.

In the centre of Driffield lies ***The Bell Hotel***, a traditional coaching inn that dates back to the early 1700s. The earliest recorded landlord was a William Porter who also promoted the canal which eventually linked Driffield with Hull and brought prosperity to the

The Bell Hotel

town. At that time, the courtyard opened onto the main street through an arch and the stables were located where the car park is now. In Victorian times the name was changed from *"The Blue Bell"* to *"The Bell Hotel"* and the archway was closed off.

The establishment has been privately owned for most of its lifetime and for the last 22 years has been run by Mr Riggs. The Bell is renowned throughout the area, and beyond, as being one of the premier hotels in this part of Yorkshire and it certainly lives up to its reputation. Throughout the hotel much of the decor retains the building's original features, in particular the wood panelling in the Oak Room and billiard room, and the plasterwork in the hall. The 14 bedrooms continue the standards of decor, all are en suite, and some feature four-poster beds.

However, the main reason that guests return again and again to The Bell is the outstanding cuisine. Whether choosing something from the lunchtime buffet or sitting in the dining room and selecting from the a la carte menu, no diner will be disappointed. Traditionally styled, the complex provides a spacious and luxurious environment exclusively for the enjoyment of hotel guests. Here, guests will find a swimming pool, whirlpool, sauna and steam room. The Bell is ideally situated to use as a base for touring and is equally impressive if used as a brief stop for refreshment. *The Bell Hotel, Market Place, Driffield, East Yorkshire, YO25 7AP. Tel: 01377 256661*

Standing on Market Walk, just 50 metres from Driffield's main street, is the outstanding ***Harlequin Restaurant***. Owned for the past three years by Angela and Raymond Simpson, this first class establishment is tastefully decorated, with clowns used as the main

The Harlequin Restaurant

decorative theme. The menu is extensive, catering for all tastes, with the emphasis on English and Continental dishes. The results are delicious and surprisingly well-priced. If you have room after sampling one of the many hot and cold starters and a main course, there is always a tantalisingly selection of sweets including such delights as Chocolate Fritters or Deep Fried Banana with Butterscotch Sauce. The restaurant is open for lunch, and in the evening Tuesday to Saturday, and seats just 30 diners - it is recommended that you book for Friday and Saturday to avoid disappointment. Vegetarians are well-catered for and there are facilities for the disabled. Children are welcome. *Harlequin Restaurant, 3 Market Walk, Driffield, East Yorkshire, YO25 7BW. Tel: 01377 240984*

Driffield has expanded westward to meet up with its smaller neighbour, Little Driffield. A tablet in the church here claims that, in the Saxon monastery that stood on this site, Aldred, King of Northumbria was buried in AD 705 after being wounded in a battle against the Danes.

The **Downe Arms Restaurant** in Little Driffield has to be one of the most unexpected finds on any tour of East Yorkshire. When owners Mandy and Stuart arrived here some nine years ago this was typical of many pubs, serving bar snacks and simple meals to customers really here for a drink. Their decision to turn the pub into a stylish and imaginative restaurant has certainly paid off. In a

The Downe Arms Restaurant

short time, the Downe Arms Restaurant has established a fine reputation throughout the area and patrons will travel considerable distances to enjoy the creative and varied menus. In cosy and charming surroundings, delicious international dishes are served which combine the very best of excellent, fresh British produce with the style and expertise of an experienced and skilled chef. Open every day except Monday for lunch and dinner, it will come as no surprise that booking is advisable at the weekend for this excellent, Egon Ronay recommended restaurant. *Downe Arms Restaurant, Little Driffield, East Yorkshire, YO25 7XD. Tel: 01377 252243*

A few miles northwest of Great Driffield is **Sledmere House**, a noble Georgian mansion built by the Sykes family in the 1750s when this area was still a wilderness infested with packs of marauding wolves. Inside, there is fine furniture by Chippendale and Sheraton, and decorated plasterwork by Joseph Rose. The copy of a naked, and well-endowed, Apollo Belvedere in the landing alcove must have caused many a maidenly blush ion Victorian times, and the Turkish Room - inspired by the Sultan's salon in Istanbul's Valideh Mosque - is a dazzling example of oriental opulence. Outside, the gardens and the 220 acres of parkland were landscaped, of course, by Capability Brown.

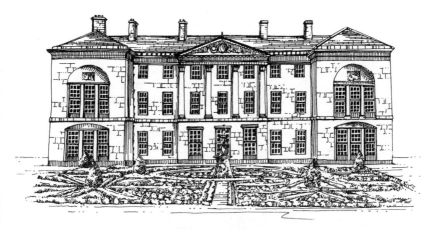

Sledmere House

The Sykes family set a shining example to other landowners in the Wolds by agricultural improvements that transformed a *"blank and barren tract of land"* into one of the most productive and best cultivated districts in the county. They founded the famous Sledmere Stud, and the second Sir Tatton Sykes spent nearly two million pounds on building and restoring churches in the area. Sledmere House itself was ravaged by fire in 1911. Sir Tatton was enjoying his favourite lunchtime dessert of rice pudding when a servant rushed in with news of the fire and urged him to leave the house. 'First, I must finish my pudding, finish my pudding' he declared, and did so. An armchair was set up for him on the lawn and Sir Tatton, then eighty-five years old, followed the progress of the conflagration as the household staff laboured to rescue the house's many treasures. Sledmere was quickly restored and the Sykes family is still in residence. The house is open to the public and music lovers make sure they visit between 2 and 4pm when the enormous pipe organ is being played.

Across the road from Sledmere House are two remarkable, elaborately detailed, monuments. The ***Eleanor Cross*** - modelled on those set up by Edward I in memory of his Queen, was erected by Sir Tatton Sykes in 1900; the ***Waggoners Memorial*** designed by Sir Mark Sykes, commemorates the 1000-strong company of men he raised from the Wolds during World War I. Their knowledge of horses was invaluable in their role as members of the Army Service Corps. The finely-carved monument is like a storyboard, its panels depicting the Waggoners' varied duties during the war.

North Grimston
Map 5 ref H6

5m SE of Malton, on the B1248

The magnificent ***Middleton Arms*** dates back to the early 18th century and it was originally a smallholding. The property has always been a part of the Birdsall estate and was named after the landowner. Beautifully decorated and furnished throughout, the pub is a real credit to the present owner, Kathleen Grayston, and her staff. Open every day of the week, it is advisable to book a table for Friday or at the weekend as it gets very busy. The menus certainly sound

The Middleton Arms

delicious with a good selection at very reasonable prices. The ales are just as good and well kept. There is also bed and breakfast accommodation with three letting rooms. One is en suite and the other two have showers. *Middleton Arms, North Grimston, Malton, North Yorkshire, YO17 8AX. Tel: 01944 768255*

A few miles to the south of North Grimston, a minor road off the B1248 leads to one of the most haunting sights in the county, - the deserted medieval village of **Wharram Percy**. There had been a settlement here for some 5,000 years but by the late 1400s the village stood abandoned. For a while the church continued to serve the surrounding hamlets but in time, that too became a ruin. The manor house of the Percy family who gave the village its name, peasant houses dating back to the 13th century, a corn mill, a cemetery complete with exposed skeletons - these sad memorials of a once thriving community stand windswept and desolate. Until fairly recently it was assumed that the villagers had been driven from their homes by the plague but scholars are now certain that the cause was simple economics: the lords of the manor, the Percys, turned their lands from labour-intensive crop cultivation to sheep farming which needed only a handful of shepherds. Unable to find work, the villagers drifted elsewhere.

Huggate *Map 5 ref I7*
10m W of Great Driffield, off the A166

Huggate is tucked away deep in the heart of the Wolds with the long distance walks, the Minster Way and the Wolds Way, skirting it to the north and south. The village clusters around a large green with a well which is claimed to be the deepest in England.

Hidden gems are few and far between, but one that is waiting to be discovered is the **Wolds Inn** at Huggate. Surrounded by breathtaking countryside, this inn - the highest on the Wolds - offers the visitor excellent facilities for which country inns are renowned. The atmosphere that has been created by owners Peter and Patricia, along with their daughter Jane and son-in-law John, is unique and unbeatable. On entering the Wolds Inn there is a characterful lounge bar and dining area to one side and a public bar on the other.

The interior features, exposed wooden beams and panelled walls throughout and the bar includes pew-style seats. Voted Restaurant of the Year (Best Pub) 1996 by the Hull Daily Mail, the meals served here are delicious with a good selection of traditional tasty dishes on offer. As well as the excellent food, behind the bar is an array of well-kept real ales and the pub is recommended by CAMRA. The warm welcome and friendly hospitality extends to the four comfort-

The Wolds Inn

able en suite guest bedrooms that provide the opportunity for a longer stay in this relaxing establishment.

The Wolds Inn is closed all day Monday, except Bank Holidays, and it is essential to book at weekends if you wish to eat. With many pleasant walks in the area, the pub is popular with walkers and ramblers. This is an outstanding establishment with great hosts and an even better atmosphere. Somewhat off the beaten track, the inn can be found to the south of the main A166 mid-way between York and Driffield. Once found, however, the Wolds Inn will be hard to forget. *The Wolds Inn, Huggate, York, YO4 2YH. Tel: 01377 288217*

Millington
Map 5 ref H7

3m NE of Pocklington, on minor road

From Huggate, a minor road leads westwards through a narrow, steep-sided valley to Millington. Quaint, olde worlde and characterful are just some of the adjectives that could be used to describe the wonderful **Rambler's Rest Tea Rooms and Restaurant** situated in this tiny hamlet in the heart of the Wolds. Angela Nesom, the owner, has established an excellent reputation for the establishment in the five years that she has been here. Within, it features stone floors, exposed brick walls and has an old range and fireplace with a roaring log fire. The Rambler's Rest is open Saturday and Sunday in winter months, and weekdays on request, as well as throughout the summer. It is open from 11.30am onwards and serves snacks, beverages and evening meals. Bookings are however advisable for the evening as the restaurant is only small. The menus for snacks and hot meals offer a good selection and caters to all tastes. All

The Rambler's Rest Tea Rooms and Restaurant

dishes are home cooked and use only the freshest ingredients. For those interested in overnight accommodation, Angela also offers bed and breakfast accommodation in one double room in the property adjacent to the restaurant. *Rambler's Rest Tea Rooms and Restaurant, Main Street, Millington, York, YO4 2TX. Tel: 01759 303292*

The Gate Inn is said to be the second oldest building in Millington and it dates back, in parts, to the mid 17th century and has, in its

The Gate Inn

time, been a farmhouse. George Snowden, a local man, purchased the pub four years ago and since then it has become very popular with both locals and visitors alike. Full of character and old world charm, the Gate Inn has a superb atmosphere and offers a warm welcome to all. Open during the evenings in the week and at lunch-times on Saturday, Sunday and Bank Holidays, the inn's visitors can expect an excellent glass or two of real ale to be served as well as delicious pub food. The Gate Inn is also well known for its lively entertainment: there is country and western music every Wednesday evening, a fortnightly quiz on Tuesdays, and once a month Friday night becomes '60s Night'. George also plans to expand and provide comfortable bed and breakfast accommodation. *The Gate Inn, Millington, North Yorkshire, YO4 2TX. Tel: 01759 302045*

The pretty village of Warter, to the south-east of Millington, is where the *"oldest horserace in the world"* has its winning post. The post is inscribed with the date 1519, the year in which the **Kipling Cotes Derby** was first run. This demanding steeple chase which passes through several parishes is still held annually on the third Thursday in March.

Goodmanham
Map 5 ref I8

12m W of Beverley off the A1079

Goodmanham is always mentioned in accounts of early Christianity in northern England. During Saxon times, according to the Venerable Bede, there was a pagan temple at Goodmanham. In AD627 its priest, Coifu, was converted to the Christian faith and with his own hands destroyed the heathen shrine. Coifu's conversion so impressed Edwin, King of Northumbria, that he also was baptised and made Christianity the official religion of his kingdom. Other versions of the story attribute King Edwin's conversion to a different cause. They say he was hopelessly enamoured of the beautiful Princess Aethelburh, daughter of the King of Kent. Aethelburh, however, was a Christian and she refused to marry Edwin until he too had adopted her faith.

The Goodmanham Arms, in the heart of this picturesque village, is a charming, family run free house where excellent hospitality and a warm welcome are the key ingredients for the continued success of this pub. The building itself adds to the charm: full of character, it was rebuilt at the turn of the century and many of the original features are still to be seen. The Goodmanham Arms is still at the centre of village life and is the place where people congregate to chat and relax and also to partake of a refreshing glass or two from the super selection of real ales. Though closed at lunch-time from Monday to Thursday, the evenings and weekends are busy and patrons can also try the delicious snacks and sandwiches. Sundays

The Goodmanham Arms

are most popular with a choice of filled Yorkshire puddings or hot roast beef sandwiches always available. Finally, the host and hostess, Richard and Pauline Akester, also have a comfortable room for overnight guests. *Goodmanham Arms, Goodmanham, York, East Yorkshire, YO4 3JA. Tel: 01430 873849*

To the northwest of Goodmanham is **Londesborough Park**, a 400 acre estate which was once owned by the legendary railway entrepreneur, George Hudson. He had the York to Market Weighton railway diverted here so that he could build himself a comfortable private station. The railway has now disappeared but part of its route is included on the popular long distance footpath, the Wolds Way.

A couple of miles south of Goodmanham, is **Market Weighton**, a busy little town where mellow 18th century houses cluster around an early Norman church. Buried somewhere in the churchyard, is William Bradley who was born at Market Weighton in 1787 and grew up to become the tallest man in England. He stood 7 feet 8 inches high and weighed 27 stones. William made a fortune by travelling the country and placing himself on display. He was even received at Court by George III who, taking a fancy to the giant, gave him a huge gold watch to wear across his chest.

Middleton-on-the-Wolds

Map 5 ref I8

8m SW of Great Driffield, on the A163

Hidden away in picturesque Middleton with its village green and pond surrounded by white-painted cottages is the outstanding **Rose and Crown** public house. Owned and personally run by Debbie and Geoff for the last four and a half years, news of their excellent establishment has spread far and wide. This beautiful free house, a

The Rose and Crown

former coaching inn, is full of atmosphere and is a place where locals and visitors can enjoy the very best an English pub can offer. As well as serving a range of fine ales, the Rose and Crown has a wonderful restaurant - soon to be enlarged - with a varied and interesting menu supplemented by a mouthwatering selection of daily specials. Although the restaurant is very popular, particularly over the weekend when booking is advisable, meals can be taken throughout this comfortable public house. *The Rose and Crown, 10 Chapel Lane, Middleton-on-the-Wolds, East Yorkshire, YO25 9UE. Tel: 01377 217333*

CHAPTER EIGHT
Beverley & Holderness

Beverley Minster

Chapter 8 - Area Covered

For precise location of places please refer to the colour maps found at the rear of the book.

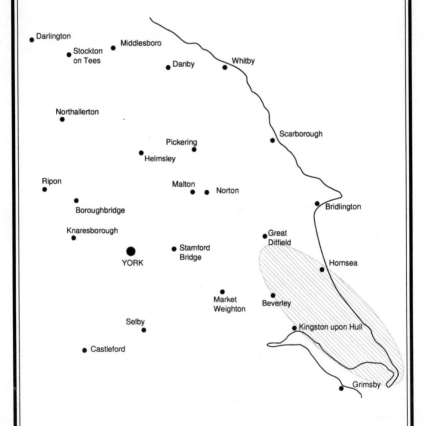

8
Beverley & Holderness

Introduction

This southeastern corner of Yorkshire tends to be overlooked by many visitors. If only they knew what they were missing. Beverley is one of the most beguiling of Yorkshire towns and its Minster one of the greatest glories of Gothic architecture. Its parish church, built by a medieval guild, rivals the Minster in its grandeur and in its colourful interior. The whole town has the indefinable dignity you might expect from a community that was an capital of the East Riding in former days when Hull, just six miles to the south, was still a rather scruffy little port.

To the east and south of Beverley lies the old Land of Holderness, its character quite different from anywhere else in Yorkshire. A wide plain, it stretches to the coast where for eons the land has been fighting an incessant, and losing, battle against the onslaught of North Sea billows. The whole length of the Holderness coast is being eroded at an average rate of three inches a year, but in some locations up to three feet or more gets gnawn away. At its southernmost tip, Spurn Point curls around the mouth of the Humber estuary, a cruelly exposed tip of land whose contours get re-arranged after every winter storm. The coastal towns and villages have a bleached and scoured look to them, perhaps a little forbidding at first. It doesn't take long however for visitors to succumb to the appeal of this region of wide vistas, secluded villages and lonely shores.

Beverley

"For those who do not know this town, there is a great surprise in store...Beverley is made for walking and living in". Such was the considered opinion of the late Poet Laureate, John Betjeman. In medieval times, Beverley was one of England's most prosperous towns and it remains one of the most gracious. Its greatest glory is the **Minster** whose twin towers, built in glowing magnesian limestone, soar above this, the oldest town in East Yorkshire. More than two centuries in the making, from around 1220 to 1450, the Minster

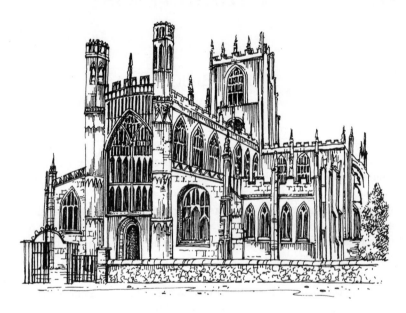

Beverley Minster

provides a textbook demonstration of the evolving architectural styles of those years. Amongst its many treasures are superb, fine wood carvings from the Ripon school, and a thousand year old *"fridstol"*, or sanctuary seat. Carved from a single block of stone, the fridstol is a relic from the earlier Saxon church on this site. Under Saxon law, the fridstol provided refuge for any offender who managed to reach it. The canons would then try to resolve the dispute between the fugitive and his pursuer. If after thirty days no solution had been found, the seeker of sanctuary was then given safe escort to the county boundary or the nearest port. The custom survived right up until Henry VIII's closure of the monasteries. Unlike the plain-cut fridstol, the canopy of the 14th century Percy Shrine is prodigal in its ornamentation - 'the finest piece of work of the finest craftsmen of the finest period in British building'. The behaviour of some visitors to this glorious Shrine was not, it seems, always as reverent as it might have been. When Celia Fiennes toured the Minster in 1697 she recorded that the tomb of Great Percy, Earle of Northumberland was *"a little fallen in and a hole so bigg as many put their hands in and touch'd the body which was much of it entire"*. Great Percy's remains are now decently concealed once again.

As well as the incomparable stone carvings on the shrine, the Minster also has a wealth of wonderful carvings in wood. Seek out those representing Stomach Ache, Toothache, Sciatica and Lumbago - four afflictions probably almost as fearsome to medieval people as the Four Riders of the Apocalypse.

Under the shadow of the Minster, in Highgate, there is a real find, the labyrinth of shops and small retail units collectively known as *'And Albert'*. One of the first things that attracts visitors to this fascinating Victorian arcade is the imaginative 3-D sign which hangs on the wall to the right of the doorway. This shows a dozen of the shops in miniature and has a charming *"doll's house"* quality, reminiscent of one of Richard Hamilton's pop art creations. Inside, the building has the compelling atmosphere of an Arabian bazaar. The air is filled with such evocative aromas as freshly ground coffee, perfumed candles and newly worked leather, adding to the feeling that one is entering a vast Aladdin's Cave.

All three storeys are overflowing with a fascinating array of crafts and artefacts, some produced locally, some originating from as far away as Africa and the Far East. Altogether, there are 25 shop units offering an astonishing variety of high quality products of every description.

The shop called Magpie stocks a beautiful selection of cards, clocks, candles and gifts, and in its upstairs room is a fascinating range of etchings from the antique print shop. An interesting range of plants, terracotta pots and frost-proof planters can be found throughout the whole building. Those interested in studio glass and crystal cutting should look out for the Little Glass Studio, and upstairs, a unique range of hand made and imported jewellery is on view at Sirocco. The Africana Room imports batiks from Uganda, paintings from Tanzania, and tapestries from Lesotho and the Transkei, while Turning World sells top quality hand-worked wooden bowls and giftware.

Leather Craft specialises in belts and leatherware made from the finest British hides, and at Quilling Cards beautiful hand made stationery and cards can be personalised by their helpful staff. Those interested in minerals and semi-precious stones should head for Merlin's Crystal Cave, and collectors of second-hand books should seek out Books on the first floor. Also on this floor are The Honey Pot and Reflections, shops which offer a varied choice of original gift ideas including framed prints, mirrors and clocks. For anyone looking for fine linen, lace and beadwork, Broderies is a must, whilst those with a fascination for beautifully detailed miniature buildings should look for the premises run by M. James. The Sugar Craft Shop stocks everything for the cake decorator and sugar craft artists, and mouthwatering, home made fudge and chocolates are available at Hideaway Wood. Also on view is a display of kitchens and kitchen furniture

"And Albert"

by Stirling and Jones Traditional Interiors. Fortunately, the Butler's Parlour, Victorian Tea and Coffee Rooms, offers excellent refreshments including delicious home made cakes, sandwiches and light meals, along with speciality teas and coffees.

The proprietor of 'And Albert' is Cottingham-born David Murden. After completing a Master's degree in clinical psychology his intention was to return to the area to practise his chosen profession. His plans were changed however when he discovered that in Beverley a number of small traders were being prevented from obtaining retail premises because of the inflated rents brought on by the property boom. He then took up an offer to purchase the premises on Highgate and set out to convert the building for use as a Victorian arcade while still practising as a psychologist. This plan was not without its problems, - the building turned out to require a substantial amount of reconstruction work which led to a great deal of financial pressure being placed on David's shoulders. However, by the end of

1987 the project was successfully completed and the building opened its doors to the public for the first time.

Such has been the success of the project since then that David has opened a second 'And Albert' in York's Stonegate, although this new operation differs from the first in that it is run as a large retail unit rather than as a number of small ones. The York shop also acts as a showroom and test market for David's latest project - the 'And Albert' World Crafts Trade Warehouse at Market Weighton, where a huge variety of traditional crafts and modern artefacts are imported from the Third World to sell to the trade. What is perhaps even more incredible is that David is not satisfied merely to involve himself with the UK end of the operation. He also travels to such countries as Nigeria, Niger, Ghana, Cambodia, Burma, Java and Bali on buying expeditions for the warehouse. Part entrepreneur and part adventurer, David's exploits will undoubtedly lead to further successful and worthwhile enterprises in the future. *'And Albert', 33 Highgate, Beverley, East Yorkshire, HU17 0DN. Tel: 01482 870032*

Close by is the **North Bar**, the only one of the town's five medieval gatehouses to have survived. Unlike many towns in the Middle Ages, Beverley did not have an encircling wall. Instead, the town fathers had a deep ditch excavated around it so that all goods had to pass through one of the gates and pay a toll. North Bar was built in 1409 and, with headroom of little more than ten feet, is something of a traffic hazard, albeit a very attractive one. Next door is Bar House, in which Charles I and his sons stayed in the 1630s. Another visitor to the town, famous for very different reasons, was the highwayman Dick Turpin who, in 1739, was brought before a magistrates' hearing conducted at one of the town's inns. That inn has long since gone and its site is now occupied by the Beverley Arms.

The Beverley Arms, a Forte Hotel, stands proudly opposite the impressive St Mary's Church in North Bar Within. Over three hundred years old, the Beverley Arms is the principal inn of this former capital of the East Riding of Yorkshire. Today, it is still a centre of social life in the area and offers a warm welcome to travellers and visitors. The Hotel boasts 55 bedrooms, all comfortably furnished and with private bathrooms and full facilities. There are also two suites. The downstairs lounge area is an ideal place for guests to relax with a cup of tea or light snack at any time of the day. There are two bars: the Elwell Bar where you can enjoy some local ale and the Turpin Bar which is more intimate and ideal for a pre-dinner drink. The Beverley Arms restaurant can offer fixed price and sea-

The Beverley Arms

sonal menus which feature traditional fayre and local specialities. *The Beverley Arms, North Bar Within, Beverley, East Yorkshire, HU17 8DP. Tel: 01482 869241 / Fax: 01482 870907*

St Mary's Church, just across the road from the Beverley Arms, tends to be overshadowed by the glories of Beverley's Minster. But this is another superb medieval building, richly endowed with fine carvings, - many brightly coloured, - and striking sculptures. A series of ceiling panels depicts all the Kings of England from Sigebert (623-37) to Henry VI. Originally, four legendary kings were also included, but one of them was replaced in recent times by a portrait of George VI. Lewis Carroll visited St Mary's when he stayed with friends in the town and was very taken with a stone carving of a rabbit - the inspiration, it is believed, for the March Hare in Alice in Wonderland. Certainly the carving bears an uncanny resemblance to Tenniel's famous drawing of the Mad Hatter.

Situated in the heart of this historic town is a wonderful hidden place, - **Ginger's** tea rooms. Owned by Malcolm and Molly Todd and personally run by their daughter Fiona, this popular establishment has an enviable reputation for the high standard of the food served and the quality of service which is offered. Be sure to sample the delicious home made quiches, pastries, cakes and cheesecakes, made on the premises by Mark, their expert chef. They truly are superb

Ginger's Tea Rooms

and offer very good value for money. *Ginger's, Swaby's Yard, Beverley, East Yorkshire, HU17 9BZ. Tel: 01482 882919*

Beverley can boast three separate museums. The **Beverley Art Gallery and Museum** contains a variety of local antiquities, Victorian bygones and works by the noted local artist, F.W. Elwell RA; the **East Yorkshire Regimental Museum** has six rooms of exhibits chronicling the area's long association with the regiment, and the **Museum of Army Transport** in Flamingate includes an intriguing variety of vehicles. They range from the wagon in which Lord Roberts travelled during the Boer War, to a Beaver military aircraft; from the Rolls Royce used by Field Marshal Montgomery as a staff car in France and Germany, to the only example of a three-wheels-in-a-row motorcycle.

The wide market square in the heart of the town is graced by an elegant Market Cross, a circular pillared building rather like a small Greek temple. It bears the arms of Queen Anne in whose reign it was built at the expense of the town's two Members of Parliament. At that time of course parliamentary elections were flagrantly corrupt but at Beverley the tradition continued longer than in most places, - in 1868 the author Anthony Trollope stood as a candidate here but was defeated in what was acknowledged as a breathtakingly fraudulent election.

The Guildhall nearby was built in 1762, is still used as a courtroom and also houses the town's Tourist Information Centre. The impressive courtroom has an ornate plasterwork ceiling on which there is an imposing Royal Coat of Arms and also the familiar figure of Justice holding a pair of scales. Unusually, she is not wearing a blindfold. When an 18th century town clerk was asked the reason for this departure from tradition, he replied 'In Beverley, Justice is not blind'.

Housed within a 400 year old listed building, just a few minutes walk from the centre of the town, is the quaint and charming *Highgate Corner Tea Rooms*. Owned and personally run by Margaret Pearce, the tea rooms are laid out on two floors, both beautifully decorated and furnished, giving the establishment a cosy and intimate air. As well as maintaining a very high standard of friendly service, the emphasis at Highgate Corner is on home made and home cooked food of the highest quality. A traditional tea room, which makes this a pleasant change from the bustle of modern snack bars,

Highgate Corner Tea Rooms

Highgate Corner's menu offers a wide selection of hot and cold dishes - from tasty sandwiches and salads to filled jacket potatoes and an all day breakfast, with much more besides. Finally, the mouthwatering selection of cakes and pastries are sure to tempt anyone who sees them and it is well worth making the effort to try some! *Highgate Corner Tea Rooms, 15A Wednesday Market, Beverley, East Yorkshire, HU17 0DN. Tel: 01482 863131*

Cairnlite is a charming Victorian family house situated in a quiet residential area of Beverley but also within easy walking distance of the magnificent Minster. From this wonderful home, Doreen and Terry Holwell offer excellent bed and breakfast accommodation in five charming guest rooms. For a town house, the rear garden is extensive, and amid the well tended flower beds there is also an outdoor swimming pool and private parking. The warm and friendly atmosphere makes this a very pleasant place to stay and breakfast is a very social affair with everyone sitting around a large dining table. A first class establishment and an excellent place for those

Cairnlite

visiting this lovely market town and the surrounding countryside. *Cairnlite, Wood Lane, Beverley, East Yorkshire, HU17 8BS. Tel: 01482 867494*

From Beverley, serious walkers might care to follow some or all of the 15 mile ***Hudson Way***, a level route that follows the track of the old railway from Beverley to Market Weighton. The Hudson Way wanders through the Wolds, sometimes deep in a cutting, sometimes high on an embankment, past an old windmill near Etton and through eerily abandoned stations.

Around Beverley

Tickton   *Map 6 ref K9*
2m NE of Beverley, off the A1035

The magnificent **Crown and Anchor** stands proudly beside the River Hull at Hull Bridge, near Tickton. The appearance both inside and out goes hand in hand with its setting and position which is delightful, particularly in summer months when there is lots of river traffic. Inside the inn are a number of alcoves which make up the main bar area, a games room and, up a couple of steps, a restaurant which look out over the river. Sarah and Lee Chester are the landlady and landlord and they are particularly proud of their popular establishment. It is decorated and furnished to a high quality, the atmosphere is friendly and the staff are happy and helpful. The inn is renowned for its food as well as well-kept ales from the

The Crown and Anchor

Mansfield Brewery Company. As well as the printed menu, which offers an excellent selection of starters, main courses and desserts, daily specials are written up on a blackboard. The style is that of traditional pub fare with some more exotic dishes as well. The portions are of a good size and the meals are very reasonably priced. The gardens and terraces are by the river bank and are delightful in summer. Bookings for the restaurant are taken for Monday to Thursday, but not for weekends.

To one side of the pub is a small camping and caravan park which can accommodate up to six tourers. Facilities include electric hookups, water and a children's play area. The Crown and Anchor can be found by taking the A1035 out of Beverley towards Bridlington. After about two miles, turn right at the Tickton village sign and immediately right again. The pub lies at the end of this road. *The Crown and Anchor, Hull Bridge, Nr. Tickton, East Yorkshire, HU17 9RY Tel: 01964 542816*

Wansford   Map 6 ref K7
3m SE of Great Driffield, on the B1249
For most of the short journey from Great Driffield to Wansford, the River Hull, the Driffield canal and the B1249 run companionably alongside each other. The village church is one of the many built by Sir Tatton Sykes of Sledmere House between the 1860s and his death in 1913. In all, Sir Tatton spent £2 million erecting schools and churches in his extensive estates.

Once part of the Sledmere estate and a former farmhouse, the **Trout Inn** stands in Wansford, just a couple of miles out of Driffield and very near one of the best trout farms in the county. Keith Robinson has lived at the Trout Inn for over 28 years and, together with his wife Marie, became the owner just 12 years ago. Together they have created a public house and restaurant with a reputation that reaches far and wide. The interior of the inn retains many of the original Victorian features, with large rooms and high ceilings, all tastefully decorated and furnished. The inn is open daily, Monday to Saturday, - rather unusually not having a licence for Sunday. Food is available each lunchtime and evening with a good range of dishes from which to choose. The homely atmosphere and excellent

The Trout Inn

service make this a delightful place to try. *The Trout Inn, Wansford, Nr. Driffield, East Yorkshire, YO25 8NX. Tel: 01377 254204*

From Wansford, follow the B1249 for a couple of miles southwards, then turn left for **Cruckley Animal Farm**. Enormously popular with children, this 60-acre working farm is home to more than fifty varieties of farm animals. Amongst them are endangered species of cows, pigs and sheep, - Cruckley is the only farm park in East Yorkshire approved by the Rare Breed Survival Trust. There are daily milking demonstrations, seasonal events such as sheep-clipping and harvesting, and a children's paddock with hand-reared small animals where the undoubted star is Cecil the Vietnamese pot-bellied pig.

Beeford   *Map 6 ref L7*
7m SE of Great Driffield, at the junction of the B1249 and A165

Beeford is an unassuming village with a main street stretching for a mile or more. Here you'll find **The Tiger Inn** pub and restaurant, a lovely old English inn which maintains the tradition of sending the traveller on his or her way after excellent refreshment. Relax-

The Tiger Inn

ing and comfortable inside, Anne and Nigel have been at the pub for almost a year and have established an enviable reputation for serving well-kept ales as well as offering a variety of delicious, home made dishes. Popular with locals and visitors alike, the children's outdoor play area and the extensive and secluded beer garden make this the ideal hostelry for all the family. Open at lunchtime and each evening, The Tiger Inn offers a special Senior Citizens Menu between noon and 2pm, Monday to Saturday, and during the high season it is best to book a table at weekends. *The Tiger Inn, Main Street, Beeford, Driffield, East Yorkshire, YO25 8AS. Tel: 01262 488733*

Barmston

Map 7 ref L7

7m S of Bridlington, off the A165

The road leading from Barmston village to the sands is just over half a mile long: in Viking times it stretched twice as far. The whole of this coast is being eroded at an average rate of three inches every year, and as much as three feet a year in the most vulnerable locations. Fortunately, that still leaves plenty of time to visit Barmston's village pub before it too tumbles into the sea.

The Black Bull, built some 60 years ago on the site of an older pub, is very much a family, village inn. Elaine's mother and father ran The Black Bull for 14 years before Elaine took over in 1989. Lively and fun, there is always something going on at The Black Bull. Situated opposite the village pond, it is very much at the centre of village life and this is the place people gather to relax and enjoy the long summer evenings. There are quiz nights every Friday for a gallon of beer, and singers entertain the drinkers on Saturday nights and at Bank Holidays.

The Black Bull

As well as serving excellent ales to the customers, Elaine also offers delicious home cooked dishes that are sure to satisfy even the hungriest of customers. For those customers with caravans, there is occasional accommodation on a self-catering site and those interested should ring for details. Open all day during the season, The Black Bull is closed between the end of October and Whitsun on Monday and Wednesday lunchtimes. A popular place, it is always a good idea to book a table during the weekend, especially for Sunday lunch. *The Black Bull, Barmston, East Yorkshire, YO25 8PG. Tel: 01262 46824*

Holderness

"Lordings, there is in Yorkshire, as I guess / A marshy country called Holdernesse". With these words Chaucer begins the Summoner's story in the Canterbury Tales. It's not surprising that this low-lying area was then largely marshland since most of the land lies at less than 10m above sea level. The name 'Holderness' comes from Viking times: the 'hold' was a man of high rank in the Danelaw, 'ness' has stayed in the language with its meaning of promontory. The precise boundaries of the Land of Holderness are clear enough to the east where it runs to the coast, and to the south where Holderness ends with Yorkshire itself at Spurn Point. They are less well-defined to the north and west where they run somewhere close to the great crescent of the Wolds. For the purposes of this book, we have taken as the northern limit of Holderness the village of Skipsea, where, as you'll discover in the next entry, some early Norman Lords of Holderness showed a remarkable lack of loyalty to their King.

Skipsea
Map 7 ref L7

10m S of Bridlington, on the B1242

When William the Conqueror granted Drogo de Bevrere the lordship of Holderness, Drogo decided to raise his castle on an island in the shallow lake known as Skipsea Mere. Built mostly of timber, the castle had not long been completed when Drogo made the foolish mistake of murdering his wife. In the normal course of events, a Norman lord could murder whomever he wished, but Drogo's action was foolish because his wife was a kinswoman of the Conqueror himself. Drogo was banished and his lands granted to a succession of other royal relatives, most of whom also came to a sticky end after becoming involved in rebellions and treasonable acts. The castle was finally abandoned in the mid 13th century and all that remains now is the great motte, or mound, on which it was built and the earth ramparts surrounding it.

In Skipsea village itself, ***The Grainary*** is a wonderful Grade II listed building surrounded by acres of arable farmland and a specialist herbaceous nursery that has been in Frances Davies' family for several generations. For many years the family had offered bed and breakfast accommodation but in 1994 Frances gained planning permission to convert this lovely old building into a splendid family home and tea rooms with ample guest accommodation. Along with the family wing, The Grainary also has a child free zone and a 'dirty weekend' room complete with jacuzzi, double sauna and king size bed. A quick look at the visitors' book is enough to see how magnifi-

The Grainary

cent this establishment is and it is obvious that guests find it hard to leave. For those unable to stay, there are always the delightful tea rooms to try. Open all year except Christmas Day, they too are housed in this magnificent building and offer the very best in home cooking. Charming and traditional, anyone stopping here for refreshment is in for a real treat. *The Grainary, Skipsea Grange, Hornsea Road, Skipsea, East Yorkshire, YO25 8SY. Tel: 01262 468745 / Fax: 01262 468840*

Atwick   Map 7 ref L8
11m NE of Beverley, on the B1242

Like Hornsea, Atwick once had its own mere. Some years ago, excavations in its dried-up bed revealed fossilised remains of a huge Irish elk and the tusk of an ancient elephant, clear proof of the tropical climate East Yorkshire enjoyed in those far-off days. Atwick is a picturesque village on the coast, just two miles north of Hornsea. It has been a regular winner of local - and, in 1997, county - awards in the Britain in Bloom competition. Standing opposite the village green, the **Black Horse** public house has been run for the past three and a half years by Tony and Jen Myers.

This is an old English pub dating back to the mid 18th century and it still holds very much at heart the old-fashioned values of good food, well-kept ales, and a warm and welcoming atmosphere. The interior is very characterful with low beams and many old pictures and prints on display. The pub is open at lunchtime and evening each day, and all day Saturday. The regular beer served is John Smiths, with a number of guest ales on tap each month. The Black Horse was even voted CAMRA pub of the season for 1995. Food is

The Black Horse

available at lunchtime and early evening from a varied and reasonably priced menu. *The Black Horse, Atwick, Driffield, East Yorkshire, YO25 8DQ. Tel: 01964 532691*

Hornsea
10m E of Beverley, on the B1242/B1244

Map 7 ref M8

This small coastal town can boast not only the most popular visitor attraction in Humberside, Hornsea Pottery, but also Yorkshire's largest freshwater lake, Hornsea Mere. **Hornsea Pottery** is an extensive complex which includes the famous pottery where you can watch craftsmen at work and buy their wares, a factory viewing area, a collection of vintage cars, factory shops, a country park, and **"Butterfly World"** where more than 200 species of colourful butterflies flutter around a tropical greenhouse.

Hornsea Mere, two miles long and one mile wide, provides a refuge for over 170 species of birds and a peaceful setting for many varieties of rare flowers. Human visitors are well provided for, too, with facilities for fishing, boating and sailing. Hornsea is also the home of the **North Holderness Museum of Village Life**. Here, in a converted 18th century farmhouse, period rooms have been recreated, and there are collections of agricultural equipment and the tools of long gone local tradesmen. Excellent sands, a church built with cobbles gathered from the shore, well-tended public gardens and a breezy, mile-long promenade all add to the town's popularity.

The Copper Kettle restaurant in the heart of the town is owned and personally run by Gillian and Tony Cousins with help from their daughter Rochelle. In the seven years that the family has had the restaurant, the reputation of The Copper Kettle has spread far and wide. Originally, part of a nunnery, the building has been completely refurbished, and the high standard of the comfortable surroundings complement beautifully the excellence of the home cooked dishes. Gillian is the cook of the partnership and the varied menu is enough to make anyone's mouth water. Whether for lunch or dinner, The Copper Kettle offers a variety of tasty hot and cold snacks

The Copper Kettle

as well as delicious three course meals that will satisfy even the hungriest of customers. Fully licensed, The Copper Kettle is open every day, except Monday, and during the summer it opens to serve evening meals between 7 and 9.30pm. A smashing place - with charming people - that carries the Roy Castle Good Air Award. *The Copper Kettle, Market Place, Hornsea, East Yorkshire, HU18 1AN. Tel: 01964 532563*

The Rose and Crown inn, in the centre of this popular seaside town, offers a warm and friendly atmosphere, excellent real ales and tasty bar meals. Built in 1930 on the site of an old coaching inn called The Hare and Hounds, today's pub is run by Kevin and Sue with the help of their three children, Sarah, Richard and Keith. Beer drinkers will enjoy the range of ales on offer, while those who

The Rose and Crown

feel a little peckish can take advantage of the delicious menu of hot and cold snacks, including traditional roast of the day, home made soups and various daily specials. There is a family games room to the rear of the pub with a pool table and video game machine. The Rose and Crown acts as a real meeting place for the townsfolk of Hornsea, a place where they can relax and enjoy some refreshment whilst catching up on the latest local news. For visitors to the area, there can be no better place to spend a couple of hours. *The Rose and Crown, Market Place, Hornsea, East Yorkshire, HU18 1AN. Tel: 01964 535756*

Withernwick
Map 7 ref L9

12m E of Beverley, off the A165

The Falcon Inn, in the heart of Withernwick, is one of those superb pubs that are not often stumbled upon but once found is revisited at every opportunity. The old building dates back to the late 18th century and, although it has been modernised since those uncomfortable times, none of the charm and character has been lost. Owned and personally run by husband and wife team Nick and Jackie, helped by their children Nico, JP and Lucy, all customers receive a warm welcome and can be sure of a wonderful and enjoyable time here.

As well as serving superb ales, with Theakstons and Tetleys always on tap, the menu and specials' blackboard provide a range of mouthwatering, freshly prepared dishes that will tempt even the

The Falcon Inn

most jaded of appetites. A magnificent place that is a great credit to the Clare family. *The Falcon Inn, Withernwick, nr Hornsea, East Yorkshire, HU11 4TA. Tel: 01964 527925*

Lelley   *Map 7 ref M9*
7 miles E of Hull off the B1239

The ***Stags Head Inn*** is an excellent country pub situated in the delightful hamlet of Lelley. Bought in a dilapidated state by the present owners in 1985, the last 12 years have seen the Stags Head

The Stags Head Inn

completely refurbished and renovated in a pleasing and sympathetic manner in keeping with the style and character of this former Blacksmith's shop. Not only acclaimed for its warm and friendly atmosphere, the Stags Head has gained an enviable reputation for its

Burton Constable Hall

cuisine; the majority of customers coming from far and wide to enjoy a pleasant meal with a pint rather than the other way around. With an interesting and tasty menu with something for everyone, it is not surprising that the Stags Head is very popular. *The Stags Head Inn, Main Street, Lelley, Nr Hull HU12 8SN Tel: 01482 898305*

Sproatley   Map 7 ref L9
7 miles NE of Hull on the B1238

A few miles south of Withernwick, close to the village of Sproatley, is **Burton Constable Hall,** named after Sir John Constable who in 1570 built a stately mansion here which incorporated parts of an even older house, dating back to the reign of King Stephen in the 1100s. The Hall was again remodelled, on Jacobean lines, in the 18th century and contains some fine work by Chippendale, Adam and James Wyatt. In the famous Long Gallery with its 15th century Flemish stained glass, hangs a remarkable collection of paintings, amongst them Holbein's portraits of Sir Thomas Cranmer and Sir Thomas More, and Zucchero's Mary, Queen of Scots. Dragons abound in the dazzling Chinese Room, an exercise in exotica that long pre-dates the Prince Regent's similar extravagance at the Brighton Pavilion. Thomas Chippendale himself designed the fantastical Dragon Chair, fit for a Ming Emperor. Outside, there are extensive parklands designed by - who else could it be? - Capability Brown, and apparently inspired by the gardens at Versailles. Perhaps it was this connection that motivated the Constable family to suggest loaning the Hall to Louis XVIII of France during his years of exile after the Revolution. (Louis politely declined the offer, preferring to settle rather closer to London, at Hartwell in Buckinghamshire). Also in the grounds of the Hall are collections of agricultural machinery, horse-drawn carriages and 18th century scientific apparatus.

The descendants of the Constable family still bear the title *"Lords of Holderness"* and along with it the rights to any flotsam and jetsam washed ashore on the Holderness peninsula. Many years ago, when the late Brigadier Chichester Constable was congratulated on enjoying such a privilege, he retorted, *"I also have to pay for burying, or otherwise disposing of, any whale grounded on the Holderness shore - and it costs me about £20 a time!"* The huge bones of one such whale are still on show in the grounds of the Hall.

Withernsea   Map 7 ref N10
18m E of Hull, on the A1033

The next place of interest down the Holderness coast is Withernsea.

Long, golden sandy beaches stretch for miles both north and south, albeit a mile further inland than they were in the days of William the Conqueror. The old lighthouse is a striking feature of the town and those energetic enough to climb the 127ft tower are rewarded by some marvellous views from the lamproom. The lighthouse was decommissioned in 1976 and now houses two small museums. One is dedicated to the history of the Royal National Lifeboat Institution; the other to the actress Kay Kendall. Her grandfather helped build the lighthouse in 1892 and was the last coxswain of the deep sea lifeboat. Kay was born in Withernsea and later achieved great success in the London theatre as a sophisticated comedienne but she is probably best remembered for the rousing trumpet solo she delivered in the Ealing Studios hit film *"Genevieve"*.

The Pier Hotel, which dates back to the early 17th century, is owned and personally run by smashing hosts Rick and Janet Jessop. Friendly and welcoming, the hotel offers excellent accommodation as well as good food and drink in pleasant and comfortable sur-

The Pier Hotel

roundings. Though peaceful, and a wonderful place to relax at the end of a busy day, there is always something going on here. Along with twice-weekly karaoke nights and live bands on Friday and Saturday nights, there is a Country and Western evening once a week (on Sunday). All very popular and great fun for the whole family, the Pier Hotel also has a quiet beer garden and a family room. *The Pier Hotel, 9 Seaside Road, Withernsea, East Yorkshire, HU19 2DL. Tel: 01964 612069*

South of Withernsea stretches a desolate spit of flat windswept dunes. This is **Spurn Head** which leads to Spurn Point, the narrow hook of ever-shifting sands that curls around the mouth of the Humber estuary. This bleak but curiously invigorating tag end of Yorkshire is nevertheless heavily populated - by hundreds of species of rare and solitary wild fowl, by playful seals, and also by the small contingent of lifeboatmen who operate the only permanently manned lifeboat station in Britain. Please note that a toll is payable beyond the village of Kilnsea, and there is no car park. Access to Spurn Point is only on foot.

Patrington
Map 7 ref N10
14m SE of Hull, on the A1033

Shortly after it was built, **St Patrick's Church** at Patrington was dubbed the *"Queen of Holderness"*, and Queen it remains. This sublime church took more than a hundred years to build, from around 1310 to 1420, and it is one of the most glorious examples of the eye-pleasing style known as English Decorated. Its spire soars almost 180ft into the sky making it the most distinctive feature in the flat plains of Holderness. St Patrick's has the presence and proportions of a cathedral although only enjoying the status of a parish church; a parish church, nevertheless, which experts consider amongst the finest dozen churches in Britain for architectural beauty. Patrington's parish council go further: a notice displayed inside St Patrick's states unequivocally *"This is England's finest village Church"*. Clustering around it, picturesque Dutch style cottages complete an entrancing picture.

Halsham
Map 7 ref M10
11m E of Hull, off the B1362

Halsham was once the seat of the Constable family, Lords of Holderness, before they moved to their stately new mansion at Burton Constable. On the edge of Halsham village, they left behind their imposing, domed mausoleum built in the late 1700s to house ancestors going back to the 12th century. (The mausoleum is not open to the public). Halsham is a scattered community spread over an area of three square miles. The main industry is agriculture and the most important event of the year is the annual ploughing competition.

The Halsham Arms was rebuilt seven years ago on the site of a former inn. It sits in two acres of its own land and it is not surprising that there was once a farm on the site. The atmosphere is friendly and the pub is as popular with locals as with visitors to the area and all are made to feel right at home. The interior of the inn is separated into three areas, - a bar, a lounge and a conservatory - and is attractively decorated and furnished throughout. The conservatory is particularly delightful with views of the surrounding countryside and facilities for children. The lounge bar features the original stone fireplace from the farmhouse that was once here.

The Halsham Arms

The Halsham Arms is open twice a day and food is available at every session. On Saturdays, Sundays, Bank Holidays, and in busier summer months, it stays open all day. The comprehensive menu caters to all tastes and the dishes are reasonable priced. In addition there is a daily specials' board. Three real ales are kept in top condition behind the bar: Riding and Mansfield Smooth are regulars, and there is also a guest ale.

In addition, the inn has a licence for five touring caravans and fishing is available nearby. The Halsham Arms is situated between Hedon and Withernsea on the B1362. *The Halsham Arms, North Road, Halsham, Hull, East Yorkshire, HU12 0BY. Tel: 01964 670487*

Paull   *Map 7 ref L10*
9m SE of Hull, off the A1033

Paull can boast a beautiful early 15th century church and an old lighthouse which is *"now part and parcel of the houses"*. Before the lighthouse was built in 1836, Trinity House rented an upper room in the Humber Tavern and kept a light burning there. There are two other good reasons for visiting this tiny hamlet. One is for the spectacular view of the Humber estuary from its short promenade. The other is **The Crown Inn** which, situated just a mile off the main Hull to Withernsea road, is a real find. Personally run by Jenny and Ray Newby, this really is a place where locals and visitors can come and enjoy themselves in a lively and friendly atmosphere. Here

The Crown Inn

you will find good food, fine ales and hospitality that is second to none. The Crown Inn is open all day every day with food served every lunchtime and evening except Wednesday. The quality of the food is excellent, all home cooked by Jenny, while Ray looks after the beers - Bass, Stones, Worthingtons, Tetleys and Caffreys are all available. An additional feature is the live entertainment each Saturday, for which there is no additional charge. Enjoying superb views across the river, there is also an outdoor children's play area. *The Crown Inn, Main Street, Paull, nr Hull, East Yorkshire, HU12 8AW. Tel: 01482 898383*

Tourist Information Centres

Centres in **bold** are open all the year around.

Beverley
The Guildhall, Register Square, Beverley, HU17 9AU
Tel: 01482 884354

Bridlington
25 Prince Street, Bridlington, YO15 2NP
Tel:01262 673474/ 606383/ 679626

Danby
The Moors Centre, Danby Lodge, Danby, North Yorkshire,
YO21 2NB Tel:01287 660654

Easingwold
Chapel Lane, Easingwold, North Yorkshire, YO6 3AE
Tel:01347 821530

Filey
John Street, Filey, North Yorkshire, YO14 9DW
Tel:01723 512204

Great Ayton
High Green Car Park, Great Ayton, North Yorkshire, TS9 6BJ
Tel:01642 722835

Guisborough
Priory Grounds, Church Street, Guisborough, TS14 6HL
Tel:01287 633801

Helmsley
  The Market Place, Helmsley, North Yorkshire, YO6 5BL
  Tel:01439 770173

Holme on Spalding Moor
  68 High Street, Holme on Spalding Moor, YO4 4AA
  Tel:01430 860479

Hornsea
  75 Newbegin, Hornsea, HU18 1PA
  Tel:01964 536404

Hull
  Central Library, Albion Street, Hull, HU1 3TF
  Tel:01482 223344

  75/76 Carr Lane, Hull, HU1 3RQ
  Tel:01482 223559

  King George Dock, Hedon Road, Hull, HU9 5PR
  Tel:01482 702118

Humber Bridge
  North Bank Viewing Area, Ferriby Road, Hessle, Hull, HU13 0LN
  Tel:01482 640852

Malton
  58 Market Place, Malton, North Yorkshire, YO17 0LW
  Tel:01653 600048

Northallerton
  Applegarth, Northallerton, North Yorkshire, DL7 8LZ
  Tel:01609 776864

Pickering
  Eastgate Car Park, Pickering, North Yorkshire, YO18 5BL
  Tel:01751 473791

Saltburn-by-the -Sea
  3 Station Buildings, Station Square, Saltburn-by-the-Sea,
  TS12 1AQ Tel: 01287 622422

Scarborough

St Nicholas Cliff, Scarborough, North Yorkshire, YO11 2EP
Tel: 01723 373333

Selby

Park Street, Selby, North Yorkshire, YO8 0AA
Tel: 01757 703263

Sutton Bank

Sutton Bank Visitor Centre, nr Thirsk, North Yorkshire, YO7 2EK
Tel: 01845 597426

Thirsk

14 Kirkgate, Thirsk, North Yorkshire, YO7 1PQ
Tel: 01845 522755

Whitby

Langborne Road, Whitby, North Yorkshire, YO21 1YN
Tel: 01947 602674

Withernsea

Pier Towers, Withernsea, HU19 2JS
Tel: 01964 615683

York

6 Rougier Street, York, YO2 1JA
Tel: 01904 620557

Index

The Hidden Places Series

ORDER FORM

To order more copies of this title or any of the others in this series
please complete the order form below and send to:

**Travel Publishing Ltd,7a Apollo House, Calleva Park
Aldermaston, Berks, RG7 8TN**

	Price	Quantity	Value
Regional Titles			
Channel Islands	£6.99	....	....
Devon & Cornwall	£4.95	....	....
Dorset, Hants & Isle of Wight	£4.95	....	....
East Anglia	£4.95	....	....
Gloucestershire	£6.99	....	....
Heart of England	£4.95	....	....
Lancashire & Cheshire	£4.95	....	....
Lake District & Cumbria	£4.95	....	....
Northeast Yorkshire	£6.99	....	....
Northumberland & Durham	£6.99	....	....
Nottinghamshire	£6.99	....	....
Peak District	£6.99	....	....
Potteries	£6.99	....	....
Somerset	£6.99	....	....
South East	£4.95	....	....
South Wales	£4.95	....	....
Surrey	£6.99	....	....
Sussex	£6.99	....	....
Thames & Chilterns	£5.99	....	....
Welsh Borders	£5.99	....	....
Wiltshire	£6.99	....	....
Yorkshire Dales	£6.99	....	....
Set of any 5 Regional titles	**£25.00**	....	
National Titles			
England	£9.99	....	....
Ireland	£8.99	....	....
Scotland	£8.99	....	....
Wales	£8.99	....	....
Set of all 4 National titles	**£28.00**	....	....
	TOTAL	_____	_____

**For orders of less than 4 copies please add £1 per book for
postage & packing. Orders over 4 copies P & P free.**

*PLEASE TURN OVER TO COMPLETE
PAYMENT DETAILS*

The Hidden Places Series
ORDER FORM

Please complete following details:

I wish to pay for this order by:

Cheque: ☐   Switch: ☐

Access: ☐   Visa: ☐

Either:

Card No: ☐☐☐☐ ☐☐☐☐ ☐☐☐☐ ☐☐☐☐

Expiry Date: ☐☐ ☐☐

Signature: ....

Or:

I enclose a cheque for £ .... made payable to Travel Publishing Ltd

NAME: ....

ADDRESS: ....

....

....

....

POSTCODE: ....

TEL NO: ....

Please send to: Travel Publishing Ltd
7a Apollo House
Calleva Park
Aldermaston
Berks, RG7 8TN

The Hidden Places Series
READER REACTION FORM

The Hidden Places research team would like to receive reader's comments on any visitor attractions or places reviewed in the book and also recommendations for suitable entries to be included in the next edition. This will help ensure that the ***Hidden Places*** series continues to provide its readers with useful information on the more interesting, unusual or unique features of each attraction or place ensuring that their stay in the local area is an enjoyable and stimulating experience.

To provide your comments or recommendations would you please complete the forms below as indicated and send to: **The Research Department, Travel Publishing Ltd., 7a Apollo House, Calleva Park, Aldermaston, Reading, RG7 8TN.**

Please tick as appropriate: Comments ☐   Recommendation ☐

Name of *"Hidden Place"*: _____

Address: _____

Telephone Number: _____

Name of Contact: _____

Comments/Reason for recommendation:

_____

Name of Reader: _____

Address: _____

Telephone Number: _____

The Hidden Places Series
READER REACTION FORM

The Hidden Places research team would like to receive reader's comments on any visitor attractions or places reviewed in the book and also recommendations for suitable entries to be included in the next edition. This will help ensure that the *Hidden Places* series continues to provide its readers with useful information on the more interesting, unusual or unique features of each attraction or place ensuring that their stay in the local area is an enjoyable and stimulating experience.

To provide your comments or recommendations would you please complete the forms below as indicated and send to: **The Research Department, Travel Publishing Ltd., 7a Apollo House, Calleva Park, Aldermaston, Reading, RG7 8TN.**

Please tick as appropriate: Comments ☐   Recommendation ☐

Name of *"Hidden Place"*:

Address:

Telephone Number:

Name of Contact:

Comments/Reason for recommendation:

Name of Reader:

Address:

Telephone Number:

Map Section

The following pages of maps encompass the main cities, towns and geographical features of Northeast Yorkshire, as well as all the many interesting places featured in the guide. Distances are indicated by the use of scale bars located below each of the maps

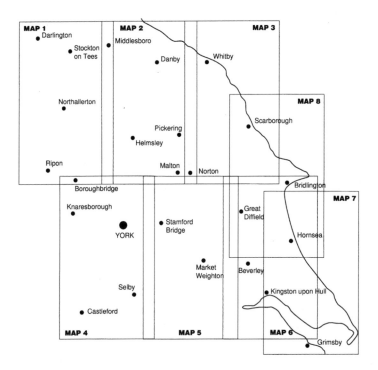

These maps are small scale extracts from the *Yorkshire Official Tourist Map*, reproduced with kind permission of *Estates Publications*.

MAP 1

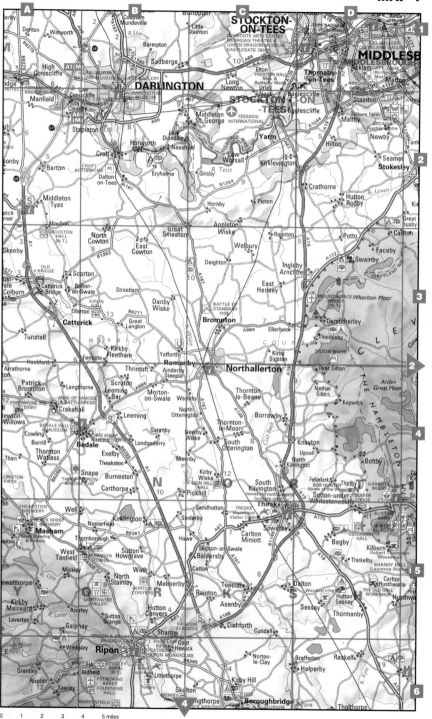

MAP 2

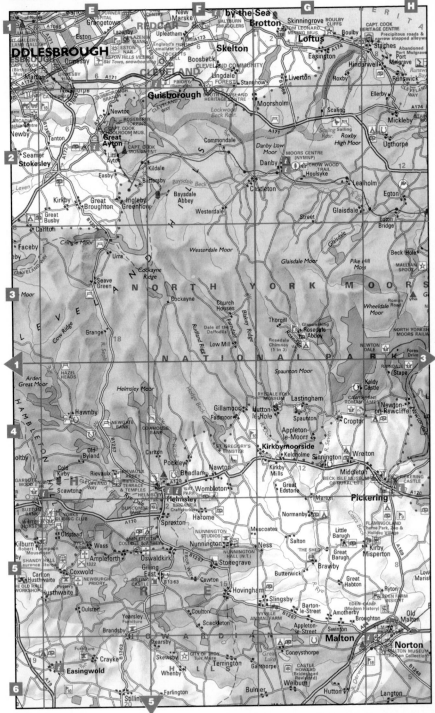

©Estate Publications   Crown Copyright Reserved